Dedication

♥

To my loves and the lights of my life—my children:
Craig, Peter, Lizzy, and their wonderful spouses: Lindsey, Barbara,
and Dan. And to my grandchildren: Cora, Alex, Scotty, Edie,
Sebastian, and Abby...and any others who just might bless our family
in the years to come. And to Karen and to
dear Preston and his partner, Tom...

**May your lives be filled with laughter and love,
and may you gather wisdom as you go.**

And finally, to my mom and dad—I dedicate all I am to them.
My mom passed away ten years ago, and my father recently
passed at age ninety-seven, as this book was going to print.
What a blessing to have incredible parents.

Gather as You Go

Text copyright © 2018 by Carol Lavin Bernick
Photography copyright © 2018 by Carol Lavin Bernick

Original illustrations: Kirsten Sevig
Photography: Glenn Hettinger and Carol Lavin Bernick
Interior book design: Amy Stanec
Cover design: Kelly Hume

Visit our website at gatherasyougo.com

@gatherasyougo

ISBN-13: 978-0-692-97492-6
Printed in China
10 9 8 7 6 5 4 3 2 1
First Edition

CAROL LAVIN BERNICK

Gather

AS YOU

GO

SHARING LESSONS
LEARNED ALONG THE WAY

Contents

"Why did I
write this book?"

I am sure you have heard the words "lifelong learning," and for me that is so incredibly true. Someone helps me to learn something new almost every day. Sometimes it's the light stuff about parties or trips, but most of the time it is about business as that is most of what I do. Other times it's unfortunately about something so hurtful to my heart that I don't want to learn anything more. But most of the time the learnings are good ones. And so I pass it on.

Throughout the book I return, again and again, to the value of friendship—with those people who stand by you in the good and bad times, amplifying the good in unexpected ways and abating the difficult in ways that will hold special meaning in the years to come. I have been incredibly fortunate to know so many fabulous people. Midway through writing this book, I decided to ask several of them to write introductions to chapters that I felt fell within their areas of expertise or revolved around issues that would have special meaning to them. I expected a few lines on how our lives had intersected and some thoughts on how the topic of the chapter touched them. What I received back was careful, caring, deeply thought-out sharing of their wisdom, which in each case could well be the basis for a freestanding book. Each introduction serves as a reminder to me of the enduring value of friendship. I want to express my deep thanks to these wonderful friends who were willing to add greater depth to this book; you will get to know them in the chapters ahead.

Along the way, I've given a lot of thought to how all of this should be arranged. But, like life, it doesn't fall into any neat order. Sometimes a crisis interrupts the best-laid plans. There are days when kids or grandkids take precedence, and there are other days when your focus is demanded elsewhere. Some days you just feel like throwing a party—and some days you don't.

So, I haven't concentrated too hard on a plan or a narrative flow to weave all these disparate life parts together. I have kind of treated it like life: take it as it comes. The "Contents" page gives you a map so you can start with the sections that most interest you or might have the most meaning to where your life is today. Personally, I hope you'll come back to some of the other sections as well and perhaps find a surprise lesson, a warning, or even a smile where you might not expect it.

Most of all, in reading about my experiences, may you find something that has meaning to you, as it all has had great meaning to me.

C.L.B.

Meet the Stars—Today

It takes a lot of courage to tell all the stories that follow and subject my family to the exposure of all that is in this book. But without full disclosure, how is anyone going to really learn anything? I want to thank my incredible family for their support, and most of all, for allowing me to go "open kimono" with so many of our life stories.

For the too-quick reader it might appear that *everything* is a problem, and that my life is a version of *The Perils of Carol:* oh, the company must have been a disaster, the kids a constant trial, and so on.

And all that is nonsense.

Does everything always go as planned? Never. But with patience, good will, and, most importantly, when you're surrounded by caring, bright, motivated people, most everything has a prayer of getting back on track quickly and stronger than ever.

My mom and dad founded Alberto Culver. They grew its sales and earnings year-in and year-out steadily, if not always in a straight line, from the initial $500,000 investment in the mid-1950s to a multi-billion-dollar international company that was committed to its employees, its customers, and its shareholders. I joined when the company was doing about $150 million in sales. Were there challenges? Sure—sometimes, it seemed, every day. And each led to a solution, and on we marched. The same is true for Glen Hill Farm, the Florida-based thoroughbred operation my parents also founded.

My mom was a pioneer blazing a trail for women in business; she constantly helped those women who followed with wisdom and support. My dad, who is thankfully still with us, learned many lessons and taught from his experiences in World War II and from his talents as a master salesman, entrepreneur, philanthropist, and executive leader; today he is still sharing his wisdom and expressing his pride in all the family has accomplished.

And my kids—for whom the occasional prank went wrong, whose grades weren't always perfect, and who faced accidents and illnesses of their own and with people close to them—grew into talented, accomplished, caring adults and spouses. They were kind enough to let me share parts of their lives throughout this book. So let me, with a whole lot of pride, share with you what's happening in their lives today.

My oldest son, Craig, graduated from Tulane and bravely showed an interest and an aptitude for working in the wonder and craziness of a family business. He worked for Alberto Culver for several years, and today is the president of Glen Hill Farm. He has added significantly to the prestige of our breeding and racing business and, with a partner, is also the head of a successful private equity business engaged in the purchase and sale of thoroughbreds.

He met his incredibly lovely wife, Lindsey, in Chicago. She was an Indiana University graduate and a key sales executive in the beverage industry. Today, she shares Craig's passion for our horses, and they split their time between the farm in Ocala and their home in Lexington, Kentucky. They have two beautiful daughters, Cora and Edie, ages three and two.

My second son, Peter, has two private equity funds; most of the money is in consumer-driven products. In addition, he has investments in tech and, believe it or not, helicopters. He's also a vice president of Polished Nickel (our family office), where he oversees a number of investments. He is an owner of Lori's Gifts, our retail store business, and he's the family's director on the board. Pete went to Vanderbilt University and Northwestern University's Kellogg School of Management; he has also chosen to stay, for the most part, in the family business.

Peter's beautiful wife, Barbara, has a master's degree in nonprofit management from DePaul University. She has worked in a couple of different industries, but her passion today is for not-for-profits. She works with one of our family foundations and is the key liaison between the family and our Big Shoulders program. She's kind and caring, and a fantastic mom to their two terrific little boys, Alex and Sebastian, ages two and one.

My youngest, Lizzy, started at Vanderbilt and chose to finish at Tulane. She has her master's degree in education from DePaul University. She's been a teacher for seven years, starting out as a third-grade teacher for the charter school system at CICS Irving Park and then moving to the Oak Park (Illinois) School District, where she taught first grade; she is now a math intervention teacher for kids in need. She is an officer of our family foundations and also has a keen interest in not-for-profits.

Her husband, Dan, is a perfect fit for our entrepreneurial family. While still in grade school he started a landscaping business that is still operational today. Several years ago he acquired a commercial landscaping business that he is currently growing exponentially; the business installs major landscape projects for some of the biggest institutions in the City of Chicago. Lizzy and Danny started dating in high school, and I am his biggest fan. Liz and Dan have two precious young daughters, Scotty and Abby, ages two and one.

They're my stars. For every single problem we've faced, there have been a hundred rewards. And I am the luckiest person in the world!

And I am the LUCKIEST the PERSON in the WORLD!

CHAPTER 01

Professionally Speaking: aka Business

With thoughts from

Byron Trott
Founder, Chairman, and CEO
BDT & Company

I have had the privilege of working closely with Carol for the last fifteen years, witnessing first-hand her effectiveness as a business leader. As president of Alberto Culver's consumer products unit and executive chairman of Alberto Culver Company, she navigated several important strategic initiatives, including the separation and sale of Sally Beauty Company in 2006 and the sale of Alberto Culver to Unilever in 2011 for $3.7 billion.

As an advisor to Carol, to the Alberto Culver board, and to her family, I saw how Carol executed with perfection, consistently gathering the facts, setting an effective strategy, and demonstrating extraordinary leadership of her board, the senior management team, and her family.

Over the years, Carol has participated in many of the family business events we at BDT & Company host for our investors and advisory clients. At our 2012 Global Summit for the Closely Held, we asked her to address a particularly difficult topic: leading a closely held business through family discord.

Carol relayed story after story about her successful and tumultuous journey. As the second-generation leader of her family's company, Carol was forced to navigate some extraordinary challenges: a brilliant company founder and father who was reluctant to hand over the reins of the family company; a company in need of revitalization and restructuring; the divorce from her husband, who also served as their company's CEO; and eventually the sale of the company. Carol juggled all of this, while also dedicating herself to being an involved and loving mother to three great children and an incredibly active philanthropist and benefactor. What I found most remarkable about Carol's comments that day was that, after describing all of the trials and tribulations of her journey, she summed it up with this statement: "My parents, my kids, my family, me...we all loved working in the family business. There is nothing better."

I can't think of anything that more accurately describes Carol's passion for life, for business, for doing what's right, but most of all, for family. Today, she is applying all of the same characteristics she exhibited as executive chairman to her current role as CEO of Polished Nickel Capital Management, her family's investment office—creativity, discipline, extraordinary work ethic, attention to detail, and caring for others. And of course, she still works every day surrounded by family.

...and some other
thoughts on business

So many of these wisdoms work for anyone, not just leaders in business.

Every year a dozen books appear—some of them best sellers—with titles like *Twelve Steps to Turning Your Business Around* or *Seven Great Ways to Motivate Employees*. This is not one of those books, and it's also not the goal of this chapter.

The thoughts that follow on business could perhaps be expanded into a stand-alone book. Writing on business and my experiences over almost forty years could easily fill such a book; whether it would be interesting or not is another question. I've limited what follows to a handful of subjects including Leadership, Culture, Resumes, and References, along with a few thoughts on Branding. Of course, it doesn't begin to touch on the dozens of other key subjects that are part of the day-to-day life of an executive running a business: strategy, operations, human resources, mergers, crisis, how IT builds the strength of all that you do, legal, logistics, sales management, finance, governance, and many more not touched on. They are equally critical factors in making a business thrive, but space simply limits what I can talk about here. At present, when this book is about half complete, the number of lessons that were not included here are noted in a file I keep called "not included...yet"—hundreds of stories. For now, this limited look will have to suffice.

Most of the lessons, observations, and wisdoms—call them what you will—apply to almost any kind of work even though they are appearing in the business section. So, I would encourage you to read them if you work for a not-for-profit organization, if you build cars, or if you work for a hospital for a living.

A few of them may even have broader application to problems you face outside the workplace.

Passing the Reins

The following story is about moving our business to a second generation. It is really a story about family business, but it is also a story about leadership and taking control. It is an incredibly long story, and the following is just the first layer in the cake—a cake with dozens of layers. Alberto Culver thrived until the time came when we sold the business to Unilever in 2011. But that wasn't always the case.

I am one of my mom and dad's all-time biggest fans. And I am incredibly grateful for all their love and trust, and for my mom and dad's decades of effort that put the Alberto Culver Company on the map. There is no way I ever would have been as successful as I have been or had the opportunities I have had without all that they accomplished with our business. And to this day, I adore my dad, and he adores me. Having said all that, I worked for my dad and working for him was NOT easy.

Alberto was his child. And most of the time I think he considered it his firstborn. For decades, Alberto was very successful, and my mom and dad were featured in national publications and won all sorts of awards—and the stock did well. All that is wonderful. But in the early 1990s our consumer products business was falling apart, our board wanted to sell that part of our business, the media was no longer intrigued with our story, and, to top it off, our stock was languishing. Our Sally Beauty Supply business was doing well, and we kept acquiring businesses for Sally, which gave it an automatic growth engine.

My (then) husband and I had worked at Alberto for many years (I had been there since 1974 and my husband since 1977), and we wanted a chance to run the business. We had earned the chance, had multiple successes under our belts, and felt it was time—and frankly, the business needed new leadership. My dad was in his early seventies and had no interest in giving up control. We underwent a board-sponsored two-year negotiated management change. It was very painful but very necessary. Two outside directors participated along with a business psychologist, a family business expert, and my mom, my dad, my husband, and me.

There is a well-known family business educator by the name of John Ward who cofounded a family business consulting group and is a professor at Northwestern University's Kellogg School of Management. I had met John and asked him to work with our family. He told me he would never be successful given what he knew about my family. He also told me that my father would likely be the oldest living founder to ever turn over a business to a second generation. He gave me a booklet called "The Final Test of Greatness," which is all about letting go. He suggested someone else who he thought might be tough enough to take on my dad. His name is Michael Shulman, and he is from Toronto. Michael had run his own successful business as well as being an experienced family business consultant, and John thought that background might work better with my dad. We hired Michael, and then we went to work.

I had to take the lead. They were my parents. Both my husband and I were prepared to leave the business if no change was made. It was up to my parents. We were tearing ourselves apart over all the problems and disagreements about how to manage and move the businesses forward. We had spent Sundays together with the grandkids and always had dinner or brunch. We spent holidays together at our family horse farm in Ocala, Florida. We were extremely close to my family socially, and we worked together every day. Nothing had been easy in those last several years. Something had to change. I came up with what I called "the three boxes." My mom and dad could choose whichever box they wanted. Of course, there would be consequences with each.

Box One: Agree to disagree. My mom and dad would stay in their current roles, and my husband and I would leave the business. Business over Family.

Box Two: Agree to disagree and sell the business. Recognize my parents couldn't let go, and we would put Family over Business and move forward. Life would go on for all of us.

Box Three: My mom and dad would move up. My father would become executive chairman, my mom vice chairman, and my husband and I would take over the management of the company. Family and Business continue and hopefully thrive.

When I tell you that these were two of the toughest years of my life, that is no exaggeration. The facilitator, with all his family business training, spent incredible hours with each of us individually and with all of us together. My dad was calling the shots for my parents, and he had an absolute desire to pass on the business to his family. That was a core value of his. (Of course in his mind that wouldn't happen for decades, but eventually he wanted it to happen. As he kept saying, "Experience matters.") Because that was a core value, because we truly would have left the business, and because our board supported the change, we eventually moved to box three. It was impossibly hard, but we did it.

My husband and I carved out our roles, which took advantage of our different talents, and described them in a three-page partnership document that was approved by our board. Because the roles were in writing, it helped to govern all that needed to happen in the years ahead. The first couple of years after the change were not easy as we had to "over-manage" my dad; but within a few years things settled down, the company grew, and the stock appreciated significantly— and we moved forward. To any of you in family business let me just say I have given a two-day seminar about all of this. I can't even begin to describe it all here, but the overriding lesson is: communicate, be willing to take a stand (as in we truly would have left), and have the support of your board. You can make things happen. It is not easy, but we were a public company. We had an obligation to our shareholders, to our employees, and, frankly, to our family. We had to make the change, and we made it work. Finally!

Leadership and Key Business Thoughts

Executive Onstage

I went to a seminar once with a top professor from the University of Chicago. I'm sure I've corrupted his major message, but I took one huge piece of advice from his session. In essence the concept was: stop and think about what you need to be and what impression you want to give at a meeting, in a conversation, or in any other encounter. Before I heard this lecture, I would make a statement at a board meeting, in an interview, or elsewhere, and I would say whatever I thought pertinent. And I talk a little too much. People tell me my thoughts are good and most welcome...but sometimes I think I still talk too much.

Around this same time, we were in a particularly critical situation with our company, and I was executive chair of the board. We had a board meeting coming up, and I had just heard this lecture. I thought about what I needed to be and, frankly, I needed to be the voice of reason. There were conflicting opinions and outside experts, but I held my comments for much of the meeting and then helped us solve the critical issue by stopping, listening to all others, and keeping my essential role in my mind during the entire two-hour meeting.

Now when I am asked for advice from my children, when I am running a meeting, when I am interviewing folks or leading a group of volunteers, **I focus FIRST on what the IMAGE is I want to convey and what OUTCOME I am looking for**. In other words, stop talking without really thinking and focus on your role, your key message, and what you want to accomplish. It is amazing how many times this approach has helped.

The Critical
Importance of WHY

Organizations tell people WHAT to do. They often tell them HOW to do it. But many organizations fail when it comes to explaining the WHY: sharing the in-depth reasons why a given task done a given way is so important.

An example at the factory level: for many companies, including Alberto Culver, Walmart is a huge customer. They have very specific requirements about how goods are to be shipped and received. We need to get those cases out the door on time,

Simplifying Business Reporting

When I took over our international business, the procedure was to write these mega books on each country. I am not kidding when I tell you that the books, if stacked on top of each other, stood more than three feet tall. CRAZY. When you look at any business, I would suggest that you have simple formats—charts or dashboards—that show you everything critical to know. I find that if those same sheets (now electronic) are used to judge businesses all over the world, we are all on the same page, literally, and everyone then uses the same tools to monitor the business. I use those same formats in board books and for every decision and action that should be totally transparent. I think our people took more than a month to prepare these binders. Why? That means that they were spending four weeks or more on something other than what was critical to our business. Keep it simple.

Building Ownership

This is a simple concept, and most people likely follow this practice: meet with your entire team on a regular basis. I found that all my executives had a greater sense of ownership, and understood all our issues and goals, because we regularly met as a management team. Our meetings were every week, and the topics included new product launches, operations issues, capital plan updates, status on new information technology systems, acquisition targets, progress on key open positions, what happened at the board meeting, quarterly results, and key sales calls. This meeting also helped to cross-train some of our people and helped me with succession planning by seeing some of the folks on a more regular basis. And as I have said and fully believed, "What we will become is up to all of us."

Never Survey Your People Unless You Plan on Acting on the Results

Surveying is a great tool when used to make improvements in your organization and get a feel about the key issues. But when you survey your folks, and they take the time to tell you honestly what they feel, it can be a huge problem if you don't act on their comments.

Of course, you don't have to act on everything, but you need to show some action and address with them those issues on which you can't take immediate action. You need to make sure your people know you heard what they said. They will understand you can't fix every issue immediately. But talk with them, and listen.

Too many organizations survey to reassure themselves that everything is going just great. My son went to work for a fine bank in Chicago after he graduated from Vanderbilt. He later received his MBA from the Kellogg School of Management at Northwestern University. He was in a training program at the bank. Neither he nor his fellow analysts was happy with several elements of the program. One day the bank did a survey of this analyst class. They responded openly and honestly. Later, the head of the program came to tell them why they were wrong about what they were thinking. By the end of the year, the best and the brightest had left. Your best people can always find another great job. If you are going to ask, you have to listen to the response. **If you're not willing to make changes, don't ask.** Don't stir the pot unless you are ready to hear the truth and carefully assess what can, and what must, be changed.

A Close Call Is
Not a Good Call

....

Business is not like government. We had a great board at Alberto Culver. Most of our folks were business people, but we had a former governor on our board who was incredibly well respected. When we would disagree, he would push us to move on, saying that in politics, the majority made the call, and it was time to call the question. But in business I would tell you a close call is not a good call. **In business, you want consensus so that your entire board is willing to stand behind your actions.** Maybe one person may disagree, or occasionally two, but when the vote is close, in my mind, it never should have come to a vote. After chairing the board of Northwestern Memorial HealthCare for four years, a given subject would not even be presented to the board until we were reasonably sure it would pass; issues that were controversial stayed in committee until all aspects were worked out. Certainly, at Alberto, if we didn't have at least three fourths of the board in agreement, we wouldn't move on anything; the vast majority of the time we worked the issue until the vote was unanimous.

Don't Wait...Act

We had an awful situation happen with our Alberto business in Mexico. We produced aerosol cans, and we sent out-of-date packages to a vendor who was certified to accept and destroy aerosols. The vendor's plant exploded, and three people were killed. It was awful, and we couldn't have felt much worse. The blame for something like that, even though it was not our plant, often reverts to the originator of the goods. Alberto had product at this vendor as did many other beauty care companies many times our size.

The Mexican government might never have come back to us for liability, but we wanted to be very proactive and do what we could for the families who lost loved ones and to protect Alberto Culver. We moved very quickly.

It's difficult to accept, but our legal system has established a "dollar value" for lives lost in workplace tragedies, based on the victim's future income earning potential and other factors. We determined through our legal folks what that value was, and we approached the families and offered three times that value. They accepted it.

We also went to the governing council of the town and offered to build a playground to benefit the citizens of the area in which the plant was located. They also accepted this offer and were grateful.

None of this determined whether the Mexican authorities would come after our company for damages, but it made us all feel better. In fact, they never approached us, and we will never know if our actions helped or not—but the consequences to our company could have been very significant and, in the end, we were grateful we could make a difference for those families.

Words Don't Always Tell the Story

I have found over the course of my career that I would listen to a presentation, and sometimes, a few days later, be surprised by something that happened. What I had heard in the presentation did not exactly reflect "real life." So, in subject areas like investments, building projects, or, frankly, just about anything, I asked people who work with me to color-code materials red, yellow, or green before submitting them to me.

Visit gatherasyougo.com to view this sample investment summary.

Empower Your Team

We had a finance director at Alberto Culver who was known to be the hardest-working person in the company, measured by hours worked. He was the last person to leave the building each evening. He logged more weekend hours in the office than anyone.

His boss had worked with him at his previous employer, and he was the same way there. So, it wasn't that he was a victim of bad circumstances at our company. It was this person's modus operandi—his badge of honor.

His staff of ten did not work as many hours as he did. In fact, they often struggled to stay busy all day. They felt bad to see their leader under stress, but also felt personally neglected and unproductive. Their leader did not delegate well and did not develop the abilities of his staff as he habitually tried to do too many things by himself.

We pointed out to him that his time was only 10 percent or so of his department's time. **The most important use of his time would be to get great performance and production out of the other 90 percent of the team.** Leaders who are able to delegate and spread the work judiciously are the most effective and accomplish the most. And morale among their employees always improves.

Be a Leader, Not a King or Queen

I use this example with people who are growing in their leadership roles. I don't like "kings and queens." Kings and queens look about their kingdom and survey everything that is theirs, and they hold it close to their chest: everything in the realm is the property of the king or queen. To illustrate the concept, I hold my arms out in front of me, and with my fingers interlocking, I then bring my arms to my chest, indicating that all is mine.

A leader opens his or her arms as wide as he or she can and lets people in. A leader who opens their territory to all, who will ask for help and allow people to share in the ownership of all the different parts of the kingdom, will have an organization that functions with more openness, will prosper with the help of all, and will have people pulling together to do their best work.

Keep in mind that many new leaders start in the king or queen mold. They want to know everything and own everything—and all too often they stifle their organization's working groups. More often than not, this approach is the result of the new leader's own insecurity. Have your confidence in place from the first moment you step in to lead. Admit what you don't know, and seek advice. Share the strategic focus, be open to allowing folks to own their pieces of the pie, and build a team that helps each other. This is the best way to serve and succeed as a leader.

CRISIS IN BUSINESS:
BE PREPARED

It's going to happen. When? How? Why? That I can't tell you, but you should have a plan. Think about your game plan now. These things I do know:

1

Always be upfront: tell the truth. If you can't (or don't want to) answer a question, say you will get back to the questioner. Never fake it.

2

Make sure only one authorized person is talking to the media. Control who talks. Everyone in your organization should know where questions get directed.

3

The world will want to hear from the CEO. Figure out the right time. The sooner the better.

4

Communicate to all constituents: employees, stockholders, suppliers, key people in your communities and government if appropriate.

5

Never surprise your board of directors.

6

Be totally on top of social media. You need to put your story out there the way you want it told.

7

Some people are far better in a crisis than others. Titles don't matter. Know your crisis team beforehand. You need people you can trust 100 percent.

8

Do you have a crisis expert in your toolbox? It's so much better to have vetted someone beforehand: there's not a lot of time when the crisis is upon you.

9

Even when things get back under control, keep communicating.

SELLING THE
BUSINESS

The prospect of selling a business is hard for anyone on the business's leadership team. Deciding to sell is a very tough call in any circumstance. But when your family is the principal shareholder, when your parents founded the company, and when you love what you have been privileged to call your work for the last thirty-plus years, it is an incredibly emotional and difficult decision.

Of course, you must always do what is right for the shareholders at any given time, and I am proud of our record of innovation and performance—the years of an escalating stock price and instituting truly good governance. The story of the sale of Alberto Culver would fill a long chapter—the careful process, why our board made this strategic decision, how we worked with Unilever to make the deal happen, and why I feel proud about how it was all handled. It is simply too much to include in a book like this.

If I wrote a page or two, I would short-change too much important information, and it would be a half-told story. So, for my readers who will wonder why the story did not make the pages of *Gather as You Go*, I wanted to explain the lack of coverage. For other leaders of family-owned or family-controlled businesses who want to truly understand our process and our thinking, visit *gatherasyougo.com* and feel free to give me a shout. I learned a lot of important lessons, and I would be happy to share them.

Branding

Thoughts on Innovation

In my early career days, when I was developing new products, I created Molly McButter Butter Flavor Sprinkles, which was used to flavor food with a buttery taste with only five calories per serving. That idea was copied within weeks by another major spice company. So, when I tell you that what goes around comes around, I often wonder how much is really new. I have watched a major consumer products company find success with a campaign for a skin lotion to stop the five signs of aging and then the same company turns around and their leading toothpaste is selling the five sure ways to clean teeth. **The lesson here is you don't always have to reinvent the wheel. You can twist a success into something else, be it a new product or an advertising campaign.**

When I created Mrs. Dash it was a hugely successful and winning idea. In fact, it won a couple of awards for "new product of the year." What was especially clever about Mrs. Dash was the advertising message that stated Mrs. Dash was "14 savory flavors to shake your craving for salt." I wanted people to replace the salt shaker with something else they could shake, and what I put inside the bottle were flavors that had been used successfully for decades—flavors like lemon, pepper, onion, and garlic. So, very simply, we replaced salt with flavor. It was a twist on well-known flavors packaged in a totally new way and was advertised as a great-tasting replacement for salt. Mrs. Dash went on to sell tens of millions of dollars and, after Alberto sold to Unilever in 2011, Unilever sold Mrs. Dash for more than $300 million dollars. Pretty good for little old Mrs. Dash. Pretty good for lemon, pepper, onion, and garlic put together in a whole new way and packaged as something new and unique.

Static Guard was another of my new products. I went to college in New Orleans at Tulane University. I had a dress that I loved and wore often. It was sort of a white crepe-looking material that looked great in the humidity of New Orleans but, when I went to wear it to a Christmas party in Chicago, it clung like crazy, and there was no way I could wear it. I went to work the next week and asked our laboratories if we could put an antistatic spray in a can. In about two days we had the formula for Static Guard. Frankly it is a quat system in a can—the same kind of quat system (an important chemical ingredient, or building block) we had used for decades in our hair conditioners. Again, what is ever really new? The idea was new and to this day sells very well in any kind of dry or cold weather. **The message is: keep your eyes open and look around you. Often there is a new product waiting to happen.**

When you think of a product, or an idea for just about anything, it is important to be able to convey your thoughts in a very few words. **When you force yourself to tell your story in fourteen words or less you force yourself to create clarity for your message.** Any idea that takes you paragraphs to convey is simply too complicated to understand. This is especially important when you have a goal for an organization or a mission statement. The simpler it is, the easier it is to remember. When you think of the advertising campaigns you remember, usually it is a tag line that sums up the entire promise. "Like a good neighbor, State Farm is there." "Plop, plop, fizz, fizz, oh, what a relief it is—Alka-Seltzer." "M&M's. Melts in your mouth, not in your hand." "Got Milk?" "The longer-lasting quicker picker upper." "The few. The proud. The Marines."

If you want innovation in your company, you must create an environment that allows for failure. You cannot be risk-averse. Not every idea works, but a well-thought-out honorable failure should not be discouraging. It can create a "success next time" ethos. Innovation demands an environment that allows people to think outside the box and allows them the time to do it. When people are crazy busy with other things at work, there is not a lot of time to think about big, innovative ideas. Provide the time, the space, and the culture that allows innovation to thrive.

One more thought about innovation and what it takes to advance your career: **it takes just as much work to create a small idea as a big one**. Do something big. Do something that, if done well, will get you noticed. Being a terrific member of a team is really important, but so is creating something that allows you to say, "I did that." Whether it's a new process, a unique-looking website, a new chemical compound, or a great-looking design—doing something that will get you noticed and help you to stand out from the crowd is always a good thing.

AVOID "CLOSURE" AND CONSIDER THE SIZE OF
YOUR TARGET AUDIENCE

When we create a brand, we think about our target audience and that is great. Targeted products make sense. But there is no reason to "close out" huge population segments if you don't need to. We bought a tiny brand and transformed it into a massive brand called TRESemmé. It is a line of hair-care products with the tag line "Professional. Affordable." The brand looked like it belonged in salons, which is where it first started. The packaging colors were black and white. Women, teens, and men used it. We sold our business in 2011 to Unilever. The brand now has all sorts of additional colors on it and even some full-size bottles are now green—attractive packaging but I am not sure the purples, reds, and teals appeal to men. You've got to ask, "Did we lose the men?" and maybe, "Are we moving a little too much away from our professional roots?" That's all to be determined by sales, of course.

Picture a back label that says, "If you perm and color your hair, this new conditioner will bring it back to life, adding sheen and body." The message is just as good if you say, "perm OR color." The perm and color example says you have to do both for this to work. Essentially, you have cut your audience in half. I call that unnecessary "closure." **BE CAREFUL with your choice of words. Closure makes your target audience smaller when there is no good reason to limit it.**

"Gluten free" provides another example. Originally, so many brands that were gluten free were marketed to only those folks with gluten allergies. In many cases, the products tasted great and were good for all people. You can approach the market with words like "Smithers chips are fantastic tasting; they beat the top three brands in taste tests, and they are also gluten free. You can't eat just one." Or you can limit your audience to a smaller group of people and say, "If you're allergic to gluten, now you've got Smithers chips." But why cut out the rest of the world? Why not find language that communicates to the entire population to try Smithers chips and market as well that they are gluten free? It can't hurt to make the folks with allergies feel like a mainstream product is also safe for them.

So ask yourself, do you want to be a product exclusively for people with gluten allergies, or **is there a way to get a larger audience in your product's consideration set?**

CREATING A PACKAGE THAT WILL
SELL AT RETAIL

Too many marketers get too close to what they are doing. They forget that a large number of their users may not read well or speak English as their first language. They forget that a whole lot of people can't read small print. They often spend a lot of time writing a back-label message that a large portion of people may never read. Every time a shopper picks up a product, gets mired in a message he or she can't read, and sets the product back down on the shelf, a sale is lost.

> *Tell your story in a graph or an illustration and limit the words.*

I would suggest instead of paragraph copy that you tell your story in a graph or an illustration and limit the words. A superiority story, or one in which you are featuring ingredients, can be told with a graph or a great illustration and a few words that can add a little clarity (assuming they are large enough for the customer to read).

I once had a buyer at Walgreens almost fall out of his chair when I showed him our newest hair-conditioner product. He was ecstatic. "Finally, someone gets it. Our customers don't come to our store to read a book. It's got to make sense quickly and work for all." Our packages had all been converted to graphs and illustrations, and the story was told with almost no words. The message was clear and more interesting, and it could be understood by all.

One more comment about packaging: at Alberto Culver, we had formulas that were as good as our competition's, but it was hard for us to achieve superiority. Our competitors had over a hundred times more scientists working in their laboratories than Alberto. **But we could win in the areas of packaging and fragrance. So, we took on the giants competing in areas where we could win—and we did.** Figure out where you CAN be better and spend accordingly.

Superior Advertising

If you have a superior product...congrats! That is really hard to do. But if your brand is like most brands in the world, your competitive difference may not be all that much. But you can "sound" superior.

No one...
absolutely no one
does it better!

Few people admit to being influenced by ads, but data shows that a well-designed advertising campaign has dramatic effects.

"No one...absolutely no one does it better." Those words make your brand sound superior, but frankly it really says you are equal. For the most part, consumers don't hear that. They think "no one does it better than you."

What's in a Name

Naming a product is one of the most important tasks in creating a brand. Rather than use a generic name, I'm an advocate of using one that is distinctive, memorable, and ownable. Ideally, you want to link the name to your brand's personality. It can make a difference on the grocery store shelf and in advertising or when searching online. I was honored to have my thoughts and lessons learned on naming a brand featured in a chapter of a book called *Kellogg on Branding* (2005), which was written by respected marketing professors at Northwestern University's Kellogg School of Management. If this topic pertains to your work or a new not-for-profit you may be considering, I encourage you to read this book.

Trademark Searches Made Simple

You can do the preliminary work of determining if a trademark is available simply by searching the Internet. Try Googling the name you want to register in all sorts of ways. It works. If it comes up too often, you may be able to use a trademark but without much protection; that's because it is so common that no one can really own it. In my mind, that is not a good name.

On the other hand, if you are seeking a new name for a brand, a charity, or any other reason and you can't find much in your category that sounds like your new name, chances are it is available. Remember that you own a trademark in a specific category.

When I introduced Mrs. Dash, I knew there was Dash detergent and Dash dog food, but I wasn't worried about the consumer impact or legal problems because we were going to make Mrs. Dash into something to replace "a dash of salt." So, two comments: if searching for a name, you may still be able to secure your trademark for your category even if it is being used for another category. And most importantly, do a little work yourself before going to a trademark attorney. It will save you time and money. You will eliminate choices by spending a little time on the Internet.

LOGOS DONE

INEXPENSIVELY

When I was at Alberto we would hire design firms for all sorts of projects, from new package designs to annual reports. The price to develop a new logo was very costly, often running into the tens of thousands of dollars. When we started our work on Enchanted Backpack (the new charity we recently launched—read more about this in the "Making a Difference" chapter)—we didn't want to spend significant money on anything other than the core needs of the program (school supplies and books), so we found a different way to accomplish our goal.

I write later in the book about doing your homework before you assign any creative project. (See "Do the Homework before You Begin the Creative Process" in the "Gathered Wisdom" chapter.) I am a huge believer that you should find examples of things you like and send them along to the design source with your design brief, providing as much detail as possible. So, for Enchanted Backpack's logo we specified colors and the look we wanted and then searched online for a design company that could fit the bill. We have used Logo My Way (logomyway.com) and 99Designs (99designs.com). Both sites give the ability to upload supporting materials.

They work slightly differently, but basically you choose a price level you are willing to pay for a design. A higher price level generates more designs and may attract different designers from their stable. They draw from thousands of designers the world over who do everything from logos, to art and illustration, to advertising. The "contest" for your design runs for a set time period, generally in the seven- to ten-day range. You will see a number of designs and then select the one that best suits your needs. You'll legally own the copyright once you've officially paid the winner and received the files.

Here is our logo for Enchanted Backpack. Of course, I am biased; but I think it is pretty darn charming, and we paid $350. That leaves more money in the coffers for our core mission. Win-win!

It's All About Culture

With thoughts from

Dean M. Harrison
President and Chief Executive Officer
Northwestern Memorial HealthCare

"You simply can't do great things without great people." Carol made this statement in a speech more than a decade ago. It exemplifies the importance Carol places on people and her commitment to developing a positive environment for individuals to thrive. As our board chair, Carol rarely let the conversation in the boardroom veer from our Patients First mission and the importance of our people—patients, employees, and physicians. She has played a vital role in setting the tone at the top of our organization that our culture is all about people. Two quick examples illustrate her impact on shaping our culture.

First, following the announcement of our first merger, Carol inquired about my plans to introduce the new organization to our culture on the first day. While I had thought of many things that needed to be done when the organizations merged, I had not given much thought to an introduction to our "culture." Carol suggested I greet all the new employees as they started their workday and offer them a memento in celebration of the two organizations coming together. This simple gesture would not only allow the employees to meet the new CEO and be included in the occasion, but it would also help reduce fears of the unknown and begin the important endeavor of team building and unifying our cultures. Following another merger, Carol gave a small gift to all of the directors at the first combined board meeting that reflected our brand and a new beginning as a unified team. Again, it made the point: people matter.

As we continue to grow, Carol leads by example and reminds us to stay focused on our people and share our stories and successes. Pride in how we work together and what we do each day is a strong component of our culture thanks in no small part to Carol's leadership.

THINK
BIGGER

CELEBRATE
SUCCESS

HONES

FAMILY
FRIENDLY
WORK
PLACE

PEOPLE ACCEPT
what they
HELP CREATE

PEOPLE
MATTER

PLAY
to
WIN-
BIG!

P
M

TOUCH
THE
HEART

Creating a Culture
that Values People

In 1994, I became president of our consumer products business, and we were in trouble. Our overall corporate numbers were good, carried by the strength of Sally Beauty—our chain of 2,400 beauty supply stores—but consumer sales had been flat since the late 1980s, our overall profits were plunging, and our profit margins, because of a strong reliance on value-priced products, were in freefall.

KEE
SIMI

POWERFUL

PEOPLE

OUR CHALLENGE

We knew we had internal problems as well. Good people were leaving, turnover was way too high, and there were some generational issues as well. My parents are great people and strong entrepreneurs, but they are also children of the Depression and ran the company in a paternalistic way. They felt they should share the good news, but keep problems to themselves. In the company's early heyday years, our best people had been pirated, so my parents moved to a "need-to-know" mentality as a way to protect our people and new ideas. You could say they encouraged silos.

In the early '90s, with our consumer business flatlining and people leaving, I asked our vice president of human resources to do a deep survey of people's attitudes. While a few of the work groups felt pretty good about the company, the overall results were awful. People had no understanding of where the company was headed and how they could influence it. They didn't know where to go with an idea. They didn't even understand their benefits or where to get answers. I was devastated. I knew I didn't want to be a part of a company where many people felt so confused and negative, so I brought together a group of people I trusted, and we started to brainstorm.

To put us on the right path we had three key goals:

1. To focus
2. To communicate; and, most importantly,
3. To inspire passion and a sense of ownership

TOWN MEETING

In 1994, within two months of taking over the USA consumer products business, I held a town hall meeting with every person on our U.S. team—factory and office—smaller groups of about one hundred people in a total of eighteen separate sessions. I spent ninety minutes revealing the issues and, frankly, shocking all of us into action. This was probably the first time in a very long while that the company's top management had talked directly to our people rather than just issuing a memo.

When I first walked into the room, I tossed dozens of pennies on the floor. No one picked them up or much cared. Maybe this wasn't the best message to our very diverse workforce, but you'll see where this is going. My first question was, "What's our biggest item?" Everyone yelled, "VO5 Shampoo!" I told them to pick up a penny. Then I told them that Alberto VO5 shampoo—the product that was running our factories around the clock—didn't make much money. In fact, we made less than a penny on each bottle. Instead of pennies, I could have dropped bottles of VO5 shampoo—the same value for us. The challenge was that within one year we needed to turn those pennies into nickels: five times more profit. Well, we got close. We made four and a half cents per bottle one year later.

CONFRONTING REAL ISSUES

It was a core part of our new culture to confront the real issues. We couldn't simply talk about it; we needed to air the issues so we could act on them. We lived in a world where our competitors had billion-dollar brands and spent $100 million on advertising. It was easy to freak, easy to think you couldn't compete, and easy to lose track of the pennies. **But believe me, pennies add up, innovation can trump big bucks, and you must always play to win.**

Alberto Culver Consumer Products had to re-learn how to compete, how to innovate, and, very importantly, how to create a culture that helped us to find, attract, and keep great people.

So how did we do it? An important part was learning how to listen. As we approached our VO5 profit issues, we learned quickly. Our factory workers had answers as to how to run the lines faster. Our engineers, scientists, and packaging folks had answers. Everyone had ideas and everyone, once they truly understood the seriousness of our issues and once they understood they were in fact responsible for their own and the company's future, came together. The walls came down, and we started to rebuild. We had to have the courage as a management team to ask for help. We had to lay all the facts on the line. **Importantly, we showed our vulnerabilities as an organization and truly started to grow.**

To recap: it's all about communication. If you don't tell your workforce the concrete truth, they will make it up: rumors will breed, and the untruths will suck time and energy out of the environment. When there is bad news, there are always bad vibes and no matter how confidential I asked people to be, some just couldn't stay quiet. I find the best way to approach any issue is with in-your-face honesty. **"The what" is important, of course, "the how" is important, but most important is "the why."** All the way down to the forklift drivers, people need to know why: how did we mess this up, what went wrong, why are we doing what we're doing, and what is the raw truth? All of this must be out in the open—never behind anyone's back.

Once we were truly listening and decided this approach was working, we needed to create a vehicle to drive change.

ADVOCATES: GROUP DEVELOPMENT LEADERS
So we created a job—about eighty jobs, actually—and this is the story of the GDL.

GDL is short for group development leader (eventually we upgraded it to growth development leader). Simply, we raised to a whole new level the importance of people in our work place. **We made the care and feeding of our workforce a huge priority.** We became over-the-top passionate about it. And we measured it.

The GDL title was in addition to a person's regular job. Each GDL was responsible for a group of ten to twenty people. Sometimes they were the supervisors, managers, or vice presidents of those people, but often not. While generally the employees for whom they were responsible were within the GDL's day-to-day work group, sometimes they were not.

What was most important was that these new GDLs had to be good communicators and passionate about what the company was trying to accomplish. Senior management met with the whole group of GDLs about ten times a year. And when I say senior management, that means I was always there, and I built my calendar around these meetings, as did all our managers and vice presidents whenever possible. Tone at the top is incredibly important in every major initiative and process, but especially when trying to change a culture. This was all about two-way communication. We wanted to hear what their groups were talking about: what bothered them, what they didn't understand, and what they were proud of. At the same time, we laid out new company plans, problems, initiatives, and things we were particularly proud of such as our charitable giving, awards in the marketplace, or how our stock was being viewed by the analysts. In doing this we had several goals. First, we needed to solve as many of the problems as we could, either immediately or on a given timetable (examples: we needed more computers and we needed better telecommunications). And second, we needed to make sure that everyone heard the same and the full message. Rumors were discussed and dispelled, new programs or benefits were presented, and strategic thoughts were explored.

It was the responsibility of the GDL to meet with their groups

always come first? Families count. It did in fact become a competitive edge for us. But don't ever get me wrong: most people at Alberto Culver worked harder and longer than they ever worked anywhere else.

We simply offered a place that recognized and celebrated the "what else" in people's lives.

At Alberto Culver, we were proud that we knew who we were and who we were not. As we set out to energize and change our culture, we had to face the facts: we were not saving lives, rebuilding the inner cities, or providing shelter to the homeless.

We made shampoo. But how could we get people totally engaged in selling more shampoo and making more money?

One of the ways we succeeded was by touching the hearts of the people who worked for us.

POWERFUL GROWTH LINKED TO CARING
Everything fun, warm, and wonderful about what we were as a company, we tied back to powerful growth. We had always supported hundreds of charities. In my company-wide message each year, we featured video clips of three or four of the groups we supported.

It was truly powerful for our people to hear Henry Betts, the head of the Rehabilitation Institute of Chicago share how we'd helped, or to hear Ralph Campagna of Off the Street Club, a nationally recognized program that gives kids who live in the most drug- and crime-infested areas of Chicago a place of hope, share how we had played a part.

We gave money, we gave time, we made Christmas special for kids and seniors, we tutored, we taught; and all this was warmly wrapped in video clips that featured a powerful message—a message that worked for our people and our shareholders.

That message was simply: **powerful growth yields the privilege to care**. Every new program we initiated, every benefit we offered, and every celebration we held was tied to powerful growth.

The more money we made, the more charities we could support, and the more employee benefits we could offer. Over time, I am positive this was key in driving morale and "employee ownership" of products and processes.

All of this works. I'm passionate in my belief that people drive everything. At Alberto, we said that we have people, and we have brands. **I personally believe our culture change was the most important new product we launched in our fifty-plus-year history.**

In June 2001, we were honored when the *Harvard Business Review* published our story on culture change: "When Your Company Needs a Makeover." Our story was later reprinted in *Harvard Business Review on Culture and Change* (2002). In addition, the story of Alberto's remarkable growth and culture change is profiled in *Apples Are Square* (2012), by Susan Kuczmarski and Thomas Kuczmarski, and in *Resurgence: The Four Stages of Market-Focused Reinvention* (2014), by Gregory S. Carpenter, Gary F. Gebhardt, and John F. Sherry.

REMEMBER THAT COMPANIES DON'T SUCCEED... PEOPLE DO

TO RECAP QUICKLY:

LISTEN TO YOUR WORKFORCE
It may hurt, but your people are talking anyway. The only one who may not know it is you—and once you listen, ACT!

RAISE THE CARE AND FEEDING OF YOUR PEOPLE TO A JOB
Provide a role complete with a job description and a job evaluation. You are looking for passion and engagement.

BUILD IT WITH YOUR PEOPLE
People accept what they help create. Whatever the process or program, it will be stronger and better than you could ever do on your own—and it will be better accepted.

ADMIT MISTAKES. TALK ABOUT YOUR VULNERABILITIES. ASK FOR HELP
People want to help. Get them off the sidelines and into the issues.

COMMUNICATE THE "WHY": IT'S A CRITICAL PART OF ALL COMMUNICATION

USE IN-YOUR-FACE HONESTY
It cuts through all the rumors and allows you to tackle issues quickly.

TAKE EVERY CHANCE TO REINFORCE THE CULTURE
It's the job of the leader. Small actions cause talk—good talk—and it continues to build. All of top management needs to be passionately supportive.

FOCUS...FOCUS...FOCUS
Cut down the list of priorities and only go after the huge ones. For Alberto, innovation was everything.

MEASURE YOUR SUCCESS
You change what you measure. Let your people tell you how well you are doing. Make changes when something is not working. Revisit those measures. Build a history. Always share the results.

KEEP IT SIMPLE
"Common sense is instinct. Enough of it is genius." A piece of information must be understood to be remembered.

MARKET IT! THERE IS POWER IN WHAT YOU ARE ALREADY DOING.
We get too close. Make sure you are reminding your people on a regular basis what you're already doing that is good, strong, and powerful.

MAKE THE CELEBRATIONS BIG
Big does not mean costly. Take time out to celebrate. People appreciate it, and it builds the team.

COMMUNICATE IEVs (Individual Economic Values)
Take the time to tell people one by one exactly what you want them to do.

VALIDATE THE WHOLE PERSON
Remember the concept of each person living for a "higher power." Respecting this builds incredible loyalty.

THINK BIG
Change the game: thinking with dream-team goals can make magic happen. Involve everyone.

TOUCH THE HEART
Make what you do every day more important than manufacturing shampoo. Powerful growth yields the privilege to care.

REMEMBER COMPANIES DON'T SUCCEED... PEOPLE DO

In-Your-Face Honesty

My parents were fantastic business people and all of our success started with the incredible accomplishments of their generation. But in their generation, you didn't share problems, you only shared victories (or at least that was the way it was at Alberto). We had a huge number of significant changes that took place in our culture change movement. One of them was sharing all the issues, problems, mistakes, and other vital information with our people. We called it "in-your-face honesty." It sounds tough, and maybe it was a little, but what it really meant was **we would talk about the business ISSUES, not the people. We would talk openly about the mistakes we made.** We would talk about what happened in the open, not behind someone's back. We also used the phrase "no dead dogs on the table"—kind of crass, but it translates to when something smells and people aren't acknowledging it, we still have trouble—also known as "elephants in the room." We have found that if you acknowledge the fact that **business comes complete with endless problems that we are all here to help solve**, the walls can come down and people can begin to work as a team. Honesty works, and with it the organization can accomplish just about anything.

Growth Happens: Change from Within

One of the keys to Alberto's culture makeover was to ensure all our team members knew we would listen to their ideas and implement those that made sense. The concept of the following process was to **encourage our people to help us grow**. We used our GDLs (group development leaders) for this process through an exercise that we called "four corners."

Regularly, we asked our GDLs (about eighty of them) what issues were impacting their groups and limiting our growth. Once a year, and the date varied, we "formalized" that process by devoting an entire meeting to the major issues and irritants about which their groups were buzzing. We divided the GDLs, and any guests who were accompanying them, into four groups and sent them to the corners of the meeting room; to keep friends (or advocates) from clustering together, we randomly assigned numbers one through four to seats before the meeting. Then we asked them specifically to list: 1) the things that irritated them most about the workplace—we called these micros, and 2) their suggestions for major changes that could make a difference for us going forward—we called these macros. Everything was on the table at this point, from benefits to policies to acquisitions. We asked them to make two lists, one micro and one macro, and to put each in priority order. We gave them fifteen minutes. If it wasn't immediately top of mind, we didn't want to hear about it. Nor did we want a lot of time spent on something that had one or two advocates or that represented some personal agenda. We wanted a majority consensus.

Then we reassembled into one group. We explained the ground rules. We didn't have unlimited resources, so an idea that would take significant funds probably reduced the total number of things we could consider. **While we were transparent, it wasn't a pure democracy**—so a suggestion such as reducing the work week to three days would be a wasted vote.

We asked each group to give us their top four micros and top four macros. We assembled these into two master lists, eliminating duplications (of which there were often many). Then the whole group, with each person having four votes for each list, voted on each of

When Writing a Resume

I have probably reviewed a thousand or more resumes in my life. I can't tell you how many are poorly written. I don't mean in a grammatical way. I mean in the way a person describes what he or she has done.

When writing a resume, **tell your reader what you have accomplished. Be specific. Show RESULTS.**

Good examples would be:

- Sales grew by 18 percent in my district.
- Profit margins under my watch increased 8 percent each year for the last five years in the division I managed.
- I created and launched a new brand that was successful in the marketplace and resulted in first year sales of over $40 million.
- I overhauled a new website for our company, and it increased viewing/purchases by over 40 percent.
- I created a program that reduced accidents on our plant floor by 22 percent.

It's not enough that you created a new website; you need to show you created something that caused positive results. **It is great that you were on a bunch of teams, but you must also be able to quantify individual successes that can be tied to you personally.**

If you were responsible for opening a new plant in Canada, add the specifics: that it came in on time and under budget by 7 percent. **State RESULTS, not actions.**

The Name Game

When you're sending your resume, it's a good idea to include a list of references, with titles and contact information, in a cover letter. It's very effective to "let other people speak for you." Of course, get their permission first to use them as a reference, and share with them why you think you are right for the position. They will often play back your thoughts when called upon.

I'm frequently asked if you need a "big name" as a reference, whether for a job or for a seat on a board. It's great to use "big names" as long as those people know you well and can speak to your value and accomplishments. It's your reputation and accomplishments that are of primary interest to an employer. While corporate boards and significant charity boards are not as clubby as they used to be, they are still somewhat a club environment, and knowing a respected person from that environment who can vouch for you can help secure your nomination to join. Include in your cover letter references that will "speak loudly" by simply listing their names.

Never include as a reference someone who is just an acquaintance, because employers and boards will call, and they want to speak with someone who knows you well.

Include in your cover letter references that will "SPEAK LOUDLY" by simply listing their names.

When You Are Missing Some Key Experience

When you are interviewing "a bit over your head" or in an industry with which you are not familiar, you might as well acknowledge it. Be honest and confront the issue right up front. Tell the person who is interviewing you how you will go about filling in the gaps. Pre-think this and have a plan. And if you have been in a similar situation before where you had to "learn on the job," make sure you tell those positive stories. If you have some well-known people who can vouch for your ability to pick up new things quickly, include them in your list of references.

When You Can't Get through the Front Door

People ask me all the time how they can they get hired. They can't even get an answer to their letter. This is not unusual. Big companies are hammered with letters from potential employees. I believe all those should be answered, but even when they are answered, it is usually with a form letter. So how can you break through? My bias is probably based a little on family history, but I believe you **just keep knocking at the door and you do it as creatively as you can**. More than forty years ago when Alberto was still a very young company, a young man wrote to my dad about thirty times. One day he showed up at the door. My dad's secretary told him that he had a visitor named Mike Renzulli. My dad said he didn't know any Mike Renzulli. My dad's assistant told him that Mike was the kid who wrote to him every week. My dad took the time and interviewed this "kid," who had come all the way from Philadelphia. Mike went on to work at Alberto for decades and eventually became CEO of our Sally Beauty Company. So, my approach to "being heard" is to do something creative—over and over again. Be persistent. It might not work, but if it can break through you might have a chance to at least get an interview.

The concept here is to **break through the clutter**. It might not work, but in our family's history the "squeaky wheel" became a CEO of one of our huge businesses.

Think about something like the following:

- Can you tell the head of sales where he has distribution gaps in your town and how you would fix them, giving a detailed summary of the stores in your marketplace?
- Can you tell the head of marketing five different ways you might be able to increase market share on a given brand?
- Can you create a print ad that is more effective than what is running now and tell them why yours is better? Better yet, if the company has multiple products, do a new print ad and send one every week for six weeks.
- Can you write a PR story that is so good the company might want to send it to the media?
- Can you write a news story about the company and its good works? Make it something they have not seen before and present it in a way that shows your creativity and ability to write.
- Can you make a YouTube video on a given product?
- Are there five little creative gifts that you can attach to your letter, sent over five weeks—gifts that say something about how creative you are?

And the Politicians Said "No," So We Started Over: Introducing Enchanted Backpack

As I have said, my dad is ninety-seven. We have always been huge supporters of education, and we wanted to put his name on a charter high school in Chicago and to fund its opening. We also wanted to have a "hands-on" connection to helping hundreds of in-need kids in the City of Chicago. We were excited to do this, and the financial commitment was very significant. We worked hard with the Noble charter system, but despite all our efforts, politicians got in the way and stopped us from opening a new school.

Philanthropy with a Powerful Impact

When my alma mater, Tulane University, recently went through some budget cuts (the prudent thing to do), I was concerned about how the cuts would affect the morale of the faculty. I believe, as I would assume most university presidents do, that the faculty is key to the success of a university. At Tulane, we had weathered Hurricane Katrina, which, of course, hit the university and the City of New Orleans incredibly hard.

Now we were going through a transition of leadership and I wanted to do something positive to help while, at the same time, being hugely supportive of the need for budget cuts. So I gave a gift of significance to be used over the next five years for faculty grants. From each year's grant pool, grants for up to fifteen thousand dollars would be decided upon by a group of deans, professors, and the university president. During this time when everyone was tightening their belts (a lot), faculty members would still have the opportunity to get funding for projects they were pursuing.

This act of philanthropy was a powerfully positive statement to the greatest assets in the university. At Alberto Culver we had a saying: "Companies don't succeed; people do." It seemed to me that made sense for the university too. The gift was welcomed and fully supported by the leadership at Tulane and would help us get through the work that needed to be done with a more positive feeling from all.

This act of philanthropy was a powerfully positive statement to the greatest assets in the university.

Encouraging
Young Scholars

....

We planned a "first" party for our new Lavin Scholars. There
were fifty-four children and their families from schools
supported by the Big Shoulders Fund in Chicago. We
will know these kids for many years as we help them with
their education. My daughter, Liz, and my daughter-in-law
Barbara worked together to write a statement of values for
Lavin Scholars. We wanted these children to know what
was important to our family, and we hope these values will
become important to them as well. The event was held at an
indoor amusement park with hundreds of video games and
carnival rides. We served breakfast to their families and had
five gifts for our scholars—each gift representing a different
value. We told our new students that this type of fun event
would only be offered to the scholars in the future who 1) kept
their attendance high and 2) according to their teachers,
worked hard and deserved another fantastic outing. We hope
that this incentive will help to maintain strong engagement
and participation.

**Here's a note I received from Josh Hale, who runs
the program:**

Greetings,

While I am certainly not the longest-serving member of the Big Shoulders Fund team, I have had the opportunity to participate in many scholarship events over the last twelve years. I have watched the generosity of people interested in helping inner-city children turn into real success as these scholars are able to access a quality education, mentoring and support, and, ultimately, the opportunity to work for a brighter future. I have watched these relationships—student, family/guardian, mentor/donor, school—develop and strengthen over time. It is a wonderful bond and one that continues to show great results in terms of students achieving their dreams. Your first event with your Lavin Scholars was among the most impressive and impactful—and lots of fun!!

At your celebration, I was taken by how much you and the rest of your family and friends put into making the day so special for your scholars. The way in which you initiated this relationship was thoughtful and filled with great lessons. I wish I had a video of your speech as you reviewed the Lavin Scholar Values: **L**earn Every Day, **A**sk for Help, **V**alue People, **I**ntegrity Wins, **N**ow Is the Time. These values and your involvement, reminds them they need to do their part to earn the scholarship. I recall you telling the scholars that they could lose the opportunity to participate in future events if they failed to meet the program expectations. That is a critical and key piece of this entire program. Indeed, the framed values statement you gave them will be hung in all of their homes.

The other part of your presentation I loved was your reminder to them that they have to remember and appreciate their "circle of support." You invited them up to tables filled with gifts asking them to make choices. However, the gift for "Value People" was not for them. Rather, it was for them to give to their parent/guardian, teacher, or some other person who helps them. It is a great lesson and will be forever in their memory because of this illustrative example.

Joshua Hale
President and CEO, Big Shoulders Fund of Chicago

CREATING A CHARITY:
FRIENDS OF PRENTICE

I was asked more than thirty years ago to create a new board for Prentice Women's Hospital. I had just given birth to my second son (high-risk pregnancy) and the hospital wanted a vibrant board to help raise funds and to support the hospital, the doctors, and their research. I was a grateful patient and the hospital administration convinced me to work with them to create a new charity.

It was an interesting time. I was already pretty senior in my role at Alberto Culver, and I was on a couple of other charity boards. I did not want to be part of a "junior board" so I asked people of all ages, from their thirties to their sixties, to join the inaugural board. And I wasn't interested in it being a women's board despite the fact that we would be supporting a women's hospital, so I recruited men as well as women; the initial board had just over 60 percent men. The board was geographically diverse. These were not best friends coming together, and that meant people bonded over the issues and the willingness to do good work for a great cause.

The other key was I didn't have much time, and I was sure my fellow board members were also overcommitted; so I promised two meetings and one event a year. Our first "event" turned out to be customized "Monopoly" board games for which we sold each of the squares to corporations in Chicago. We oversold the first board game, so we created a second. The first one was called "Movers, Shakers and Makers—Chicago Style," which was basically a board game that featured corporations on each square. The second was "Chic Chicago," for which the squares were underwritten by retailers and restaurants. We made great money selling the squares and were oversold on that game as well. At the time, Marshall Field's, the great Chicago retailer, held our opening event.

After our first year, we decided on an "over-the-top themed party" at which people spent big bucks for a table and were entertained with actors and musicians; more than ten thousand (donated) favors were given out (see the "Celebrations" chapter for specifics). We brought in more than seven hundred guests at most events. Over the last thirty years, we are proud to have raised tens of millions of dollars to advance the quality of care provided to women by investing in emerging technologies and medical advancements including groundbreaking

MOVERS SHAKERS & MAKERS
CHICAGO STYLE

©1987 Northwe

Prentice Women's Hospital
Northwestern Memorial Hospital

CHICAGO TRIBUNE

FEE $40,000

With 1 Branch Office . . $
With 2 Bra
With 3 Br
With Ne

MERRILL LYNCH

With 1 B
With 2 Bran
3 Branc
New Head

Loan Value

Each branch co
New Hea

ALBERTO CULVER

FEE $40,000

With 1 Branch Office . . $ 200,000
With 2 Branch Offices .   590,000
With 3 Branch Offices . 1,400,000
With New Headquarters 1,980,000

Loan Value   230,000

Each branch costs   250,000
New Headquarters   250,000
(You must alread

HN BUCK COMPANY

FEE $20,000

            80,000
      250,000
      740,000
1,240,000

ith 1 Branch Office . . $
th 2 Branch Offices
3 Branch Offices
New Headquarters

Value

RIVERSIDE PLAZA

research, clinical care programs and advanced educational opportunities. These initiatives are improving the quality of health for women and infants in the Midwest and across the nation.

Our board operated on the understanding that if you as a board member were going to help with the annual fund-raiser and you were in charge of flowers, you would make the decisions; we didn't need a committee to agree. The same went for the entertainment, printed materials, and venue. We recruited busy people who were all capable, but the agreement with each person was: help us out by YOU making it happen. People are more than willing to help. But they appreciated our respecting their time and talents. They also committed to buying or recruiting a table of guests to attend what turned out to be the annual Prentice Ball.

The Wisdoms for Inviting People to Join a Board

- Recruit capable people and show them you value their time.
- State the commitment and stick to it.
- Bring very bright and creative people together and they can create magic.
- Work for a place that is respected by all; it certainly helped that this was the premier women's hospital in Chicago.
- Do something different. Chicago didn't need another "same-old" black-tie event.
- Make sure the funds raised are going to something people find meaningful; our money went for research and people preferred that to buildings.
- Have fun and do something everyone is proud of. You can make an incredible difference and meet great people along the way.

And Just a Few More Thoughts on Giving Back

Concentrate your efforts. You can make a real difference if you put your thoughts and efforts behind one or two causes. When you spread your time and money over too many causes or issues, you are less likely to make an impact. Find something you are excited to support and bring your passion to it.

Giving money can be hugely helpful, but I have found that the biggest impact I can have on an organization is to give my time. Using your business and or creative skills can lead to a paradigm shift for a hospital, university, or any kind of not-for-profit group. When a tough situation has arisen at an organization where I have real impact, I have found myself on the phone or in meetings for weeks on end. But then I have come away knowing that I helped a place for which I have great passion weather a really rough time, and that I can help direct and protect its future. When people think of philanthropy, they often think of giving money as the priority. I would urge you to find something you love and also give your time.

Get your kids involved. Find a charitable project or a cause that excites everyone. Talk about it. There are thousands of great choices, and all of them need help. It is enlightening, rewarding, and fun when your family commits to do something together. Start with youngsters and keep the flames growing.

Find a workplace that matches your values. Many corporations believe in giving back, and some of them do so in a huge way. Research the place where you want to work. Most organizations are proud of their philanthropic efforts, and many even publish an annual report on their community service. Do your homework.

In the chapter on business, I talk a lot about how serving the community gives great payback to a business. When you engage the hearts and minds of the people who work for your company, they become a more enthusiastic part of your business overall. You have put your shared values into action.

Great leaders are priceless. Find the best people and support them. Vet their success and then move forward. Also, be aware that leaders of organizations sometimes change. **When a strong leader of a group you support moves elsewhere, make sure you understand the values and goals of the new leader.** Don't assume all will be as it always was. We loved the president of a local Catholic high school and, frankly, supported this group financially because of him. The board decided to replace him, and there went our interest in the organization. He was a person who accomplished a great deal. We loved that. The board was way more conservative and didn't want anything to change. Unfortunately, we had to find out ourselves that the president had been asked to leave. He had been told by the board that if he contacted any donors his severance package would be reduced significantly. Unfortunate but true.

A public or private foundation needs to have a clear and concise mission statement that spells out where donors' money will be focused and why. This is usually common with public foundations, but too often private foundations don't think strategically about where their money will go. Having a mission does two things: first, it allows you to focus your dollars on causes that have the most meaning to you and that will increase the impact of your dollars; and second, while not as important but a good thing to have in your tool kit, it gives you a valid reason to turn down so many places that are seeking your help but don't meet the foundation's mission.

Small gifts can make a huge difference to the right organization. Because our company was the "little guy" in the land of giants, we believed in giving seed money to a number of organizations. We wanted to be important to people starting up a new charity or a new program within an existing structure. We wanted our limited dollars to go farther and be the funds that would help groups get started. We were hugely important to these organizations, and the money given was not a huge amount. Sometimes a couple thousand dollars can start a new charity or bring life to a new program. Creating something new can be even more rewarding.

Be careful of noisy members on charity boards. It is amazing to me how critical people can be of others' efforts when on a board, especially given that these noisy board members seldom do any of the real work. I have seen this happen often with charity events. Board members have strong opinions of what works and what doesn't, and how to improve all aspects of an event. But when you want their time, they disappear. I have found it is better to work with the board members who give their time as well as their opinions. That is when real work gets done. The same holds true for committee work and board meetings. If you want to make an impact, get to know the people who truly put in the time to make a difference.

Always check the amount of administrative funds used by the charity. The lower the number, usually the better. But go beyond the numbers. A new charity will have higher administrative costs than a well-established one, as they have not yet maximized their fund-raising capabilities, and they have the initial costs of building infrastructure. To do a good job you need good people. Usually, the more talented people cost more, and the administrative costs increase. So be careful. What you want is a well-run organization that has strong people and measures the results of their efforts—so the numbers alone do not always tell the whole story.

Most people give money and restrict its use for a specific purpose. That is hugely beneficial to an organization, but unrestricted funds are critical too. You may want to give consideration to an unrestricted gift; don't be surprised if it gets an even bigger acknowledgment than that wonderful restricted gift you gave a few years ago.

If you want to change the trajectory of your business results, you can't think in one- or two-percent increments. You need to have a goal that necessitates massive change on all fronts. I would urge you to think the same way when you are working with a charity. Define the objective, be laser focused, and GO for significant change. So, if you want to increase the number of free meals provided to those in need, and you are serving eight thousand meals now, what would you have to do to feed sixteen thousand? What could we do to make that happen? With a change in thinking that might just be possible. And if you fail, maybe you will only serve ten thousand meals. That is a whole lot more than before, and you have made a real impact. **When you are focused, you can think big and plot your growth path.**

On another note, I have also found that all too many not-for-profit organizations don't know what they are selling. They try to sell the grocery store instead of bananas. In other words, it is impossible to help them brand their organization, and create effective selling messages (read that as brochures, print ads, a website, or public service TV messages) because frankly, they are trying to do too many things at once, and they have not focused. **You need to be able to tell the world in fifteen words or less exactly what you do.** And once you have defined that, ask yourself: Is that really possible? Is there a way to measure it? The other thing I have found is that many charities have wide-ranging goals that frankly are not achievable. Example: our mission is to eliminate poverty in Chicago. Fantastic goal, but how will your organization DO that? Is it even possible? Do you sound out of touch with such a message? Perhaps a way to better define your goal would be to say something more like: in the next year, we will reduce the number of Chicago families living under the poverty level by 10 percent.

The biggest lesson? Find your passion and pursue it. One person can make an incredible difference. Let that person be you!

The biggest lesson?
Find your passion and pursue it.
One person can make make an incredible difference.
Let that person be you!

• • • • • • • • • • • • •

CHAPTER 03

A Home You Can Live In...
DECORATING, BUILDING & REMODELING

Tips of the Trade

Everyone has their own style, and there is no reason your taste should align with mine. But there are a whole bunch of practical things I have learned over a couple of decades of decorating homes. If I hadn't developed brands and led a consumer products company for more than thirty years—my career—I probably would have been a decorator (or an event planner). I have spent many weekends and countless nights poring over building and furniture plans, fabrics, tiles, and furniture. I have no formal training but have had the privilege (it was a privilege most of the time) of helping friends and family decorate homes, offices, and even a corporate jet or two over the past thirty years (and I come cheap, as in I never collected a dollar). In fact, I can claim more than ten homes built from the ground up or totally gutted and rebuilt—and at least twenty-five big projects that involved major decorating. I have, of course, used architects but have done all the decorating without hiring a designer. I know it sounds a little crazy but, knowing myself, I would have driven decorators crazy and likely rejected many of their thoughts because I know exactly what I am looking for. Silly as it sounds, it was just easier to do it myself. The good news is that once I have decorated something, I live with it for decades. I love it, it works for my family or friends, and it is decorating that "holds up." Having said that, these projects were so massive that I did hire a couple of people who work in our family office and could help with the thousands of details of all these "extracurricular" projects. The only photographs here will be my work, and hopefully the "call-outs" on or by the photos, and some of the pictures themselves, will help with the lessons learned that follow.

Make Sure There's a Focus

When decorating, not everything can be special. Let people "see" the big effect. Where do you want the focus to be? Is it the amazing floor and its patterns? If so, avoid rugs. Is it the fabric or the art collection? **Think about what you want to feature.** For this lake house, the key feature was the reclaimed beams.

Color Themes

Pick a color theme that flows to all rooms that adjoin each other. The colors don't have to be exactly the same but they need to complement each other just like an outfit would. For instance, you can have green and taupe in the family room and have black floral in an adjoining room—but that floral has greens and taupe as well as reds and oranges, and the walls pick up the greens from the family room.

A. Faux painted ceiling

B. Super deep cabinets below

C. Pillow colors change each season

D. Glass to lighten the look

E. Woven raffia chairs—easy to clean

F. Rug to blend with floor—cozy but no color desired

G. Leather wears well

H. Floral hides peanut butter

Lake House Great Room and Adjacent Family Room

Mix Those Materials

I like best rooms that have many different materials. If the cabinets are wood, the coffee table could be glass and iron, and the game table could be stone. Mixing different woods with granite, glass, bronze, and iron is a great look. Combine several materials or all of them. It adds to the interest.

THIS PAGE

A. AC ducts

B. Hidden storage

C. Wood

D. Leather takes the abuse

E. Two surfaces for books

F. Iron and glass

G. Stone

H. Studding adds a little glitz

I. Carpet takes the abuse

OPPOSITE PAGE

A. Consider a gold or silver mesh for bar cupboards; it adds a touch of glitz and is good "coverage"

Floors that Always Look Great

The darker the wood floor, the more dust it will show. Even a few shades lighter helps to hide life. I love floors of all kinds that do not show every bit of lint, dust, or dirt. Jerusalem stone floors are great. Amazingly, they looked good even in full construction mode. The only issue with these floors is that they hide everything. They never look dirty and sometimes my housekeeper will not sweep or mop them, and I am crunching on spilled sugar or whatever. But they sure do look great.

Keep the Material Uniform

Keep the floors consistent. You can vary the pattern to get a different look using the same basic material, for instance, sixteen-inch squares in one room that transition to a running bond pattern of large rectangles in the adjacent room. And of course, you can always inlay a pattern with contrasting stone. We used Jerusalem stone gray. (There is Jerusalem stone gold, which I can't stand, but the gray pattern or something like it is fantastic.) Varying the patterns of wood floors is also a nice look.

Floors that Hold Up

If you want your floor to look good decades later, you might want to visit high-traffic areas and determine how the floor has held up. Museums, train stations, and office buildings all have floors that have to withstand major traffic. In the Merchandise Mart in Chicago, there was a showroom that had Mexican terra-cotta tiles. I saw the scuff marks and the wear and tear and decided even with the "worn" look, I still liked the look of these handmade clay tiles for one of our projects. Keep your eyes open and go find something you like that can handle just about anything.

Vinyl Meets Wood Floors

I have had spaces where we had to put in a vinyl floor or rip out the whole kitchen if we wanted to go to wood. There is pretty good-looking vinyl that looks like wood (architects who adore natural products will hate that "fake look") but, frankly, it doesn't look fake. The way we have made this all work was to find a vinyl we really liked and then matched the rest of the new wood floors to the vinyl color. That way, the transition is pretty darn nice, and many people don't even notice. You can do the same thing with tile floors. We built a more rustic kind of home in Lake Geneva, Wisconsin, and we wanted wood floors. But the bathrooms and work room needed to be able to take lots of water, so we found a great-looking ceramic tile that looked exactly like wood. In fact, there were fourteen different tiles that, when laid down, had that natural look of variation you get from wood. Again, we matched the wood floor color to the tile so it all blended well.

Overpower the Ugly

In one of the homes I was redecorating for a member of my family, there was a bathroom with a tile border I didn't like. The basic tile was okay—not something I would have picked, but not worth the money to pull it out. The border was beige and peach with a little steel blue. I kept trying blue wall papers with it—as I love blue—but nothing made the border "go away" until I overpowered it with a crazy-vibrant peach-and-white all-over print. I did the walls and the ceiling in this paper, and the bathroom is now quite pretty. So, the lesson here is don't always try to match something, but instead, move the focus away from what you don't like with something that will blend and give it a whole different look.

The Inexpensive and Lovely White Quilt

As I said, in our homes I want our family and friends to be really comfortable. And we all know that those big boys of mine will jump up on a bed with their shoes on. So, I have found that if you decorate beds with white quilts it is a great clean look. They are not costly, and they wash (or bleach) well. I make the room come alive with a colorful bed skirt and decorative shams, along with drapes and great accent pieces.

A Serious Example of Overpowering the Ugly

I don't like gold fabrics or gold wood tones at all. In fact, I really dislike them. A family apartment I decorated in Naples, Florida, had massive amounts of deep golden wood. It was expensive millwork and really well done, but not something I would have ever chosen and outrageously costly to redo. It was used for every door, all moldings, and lots of bookshelves and built-ins. So instead of using the colors I would have originally picked, I found a deep brown/taupe fabric with lots of greens in it—about the only fabric I could find that both matched my taste and worked with these wood tones. But the end result was terrific, and I hardly see the golden wood. I glazed the walls green in one room, yellow in another, and in the room with the most wood, I used deeper taupe tones that helped offset the gold. So once again: try to take your eye away from something you wouldn't have chosen by focusing the eye on something else. Choosing certain colors will help tame a color you don't like. It may take a little trial and error but is so worth it.

THIS PAGE

A. Brought color to the gold

B. Added a white-fronted kitchen

C. Note no plugs showing

D. Vinyl and kid friendly

E. Cabinets hidden below

F. Indoor/outdoor fabric

G. A glass table to open it up

H. To tame the gold, found a great fabric

THIS PAGE

A. The family room can handle almost anything

B. Focus on taupe

C. Opened this up...previously solid wood

D. The gold!

Yellow and Greens Help to Overpower the Gold

OPPOSITE PAGE

A. The living room is a mix of materials: stone floor, glass and iron table, wood cabinets and trim, and stone dining table

B. Added whites and yellows to offset the gold

THIS PAGE

A. Iron and glass

B. Attractive vent

C. Super deep cabinets

D. Mirrors for a touch of glitz

E. Stone table

F. Mix of materials

G. Added cabinetry to soften the gold

Paint and Wall Coverings

Glaze painting is more durable than regular paint. It is more costly, but it will take more abuse. I love certain wallpapers and some grass cloths. **I scratch my fingernail hard (back and forth) over its surface to make sure the paint or paper can handle the abuse.** As much as I might love a particular sample, I eliminate it if it won't handle the "scratch test." I also always ask for a paint sample to be put up on the wall, big enough that I can really look at it. Do it—it's something you will live with for years.

And if you have a lot of art, white walls or any plain color walls are great. If you don't want to spend big dollars on art, you might consider a wall covering that has some interest in it. It can save a whole lot of money and give you a great look as well.

THIS PAGE

A. This is durable, beautiful paper

B. Painted squares

Change the Cabinet Fronts, Not the Cabinets

Several times I have taken functional kitchens that were just ugly, left the inside of the cabinets, and had custom-made fronts put on them. It freshens up the entire kitchen for a lot less money. Add new countertops, and you have what looks like a brand-new kitchen.

Cabinets that Look Great for Decades

When my kids were growing up, I wanted a tricycle to be able to slam into a cabinet in our home without causing too much damage. No, I didn't encourage the tricycles inside, but you get the idea. Trucks of all sizes driven by little hands would CRASH into our wood kitchen cabinets. Fine. I want a home where we can live happily but it still looks great. So, when I was looking at cabinets, I got samples of my final choices and literally slammed a hammer into them. If it held up well, it was in consideration—and if it didn't, I kept looking. There are many white cabinet choices now that have a hard-core finish that actually can take a lot of abuse. I also used distressed cabinets often as I like that look, and they can be easily repaired to look like new.

So, when I was looking at cabinets, I got samples of my final choices and literally slammed a hammer into them. If it held up, it was in consideration.

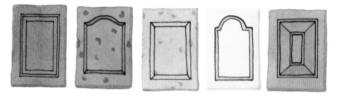

An Inexpensive Built-In Look

A cheap way to get a built-in look is to find two matching wall cabinets that you like and have the granite contractor fit a piece of granite to the wall between the two cabinets. It's a great look and way cheaper than a built-in.

Backup Fabric

I often order backup fabric as soon as a room is done and I'm sure I love the look. I have backup fabric for a second set of couches in one of our homes because the fabric is key to the look of the room. In another house, we have sofas covered in fabrics that would be easy to replace, so we don't bother.

When Building Shelves

Bookshelves are usually built twelve to fourteen inches deep. That is great for books, photos, and small collectibles, but can you accommodate cabinets below these shelves that are twenty-four inches deep? That is way better storage for toys. Consider having attractive adjustable shelves, with holes drilled into the wood and pegs used to hold the shelves. This allows for all sizes and adds interest as well.

Glass Tabletops Scratch

Glass shelves and tabletops are lovely, but they scratch and show dust—lots of dust—especially if they are in direct sunlight. Be careful where you place them and make sure you want to deal with the issues that come with glass. Having said that, I still love using some glass.

Any Kind of Collection

Collections are a fantastic look—collections of just about anything. Put collections on walls or on shelving. Anywhere. I have blue-and-white china mixed with blue-and-white Herend figurines. Collections of just about any kind of china are pretty. Try all different kinds of coffee cups, salt and pepper shakers, or miniature enamel boxes. I have a friend who collects antique irons (the kind that iron clothes) and even that is pretty. Collections of frames all in the same material or color are a great look. Use all silver or various materials in silver. Random glass and crystal candlesticks, all with the same color candles are lovely. Just about anything you collect, when put together with flair, is a great look—the more of it the better. **Concentrate those collections.**

Three different ways to show collections of blue.

The Incredibly Simple Picture Wall

My thanks to Linda and John Anderson for this one. I saw their picture wall and have copied it endless times for all kinds of friends. Take a long wall in your home and put up a running trim kind of molding. One with a little lip is best (experiment with the right kind of molding first). You can put up multiple strips, spaced appropriately for eight-by ten-inch frames. Buy dozens of the same kind of simple frame (you can find them for under ten dollars). Get whatever number you need depending on the length of your wall—all exactly the same. You simply rest the framed picture against the wall (no nails, ever) and you have this amazing picture display. I have the frames almost touching. It's easier that way as you don't have to worry about spacing. In my house, my walls have three or four rows of photos nine feet long. The frames should be easy to open so that you can replace photos easily. When we had a girls' weekend, we had a fresh wall of pics of "the good old days." It's so easy!

Think About Baby Gates Now

If you are building from the ground up and have babies or toddlers, you might want to consider building in gates to block stairs so that they don't need to be added as an afterthought later. **We have designed some gates that can be removed easily when no longer needed.** One of our designs is in a duplex apartment that included a stairway that had an iron staircase and an iron door at the top that could completely lock off one floor from the other. People could visit and stay on our top floor, and we still had security in our main residence even when we weren't home; it also functioned as a beautiful but great safety zone (no one could fall down our steep stairs) for our many toddler grandkids.

Bedroom Closets as a Makeshift Nursery

We have so many young grandbabies in our family that, when building our new family lake home, we made sure each bedroom closet was large enough to accommodate a crib. By adding just a few extra inches to each closet, we were able to give parents some privacy while still having their babies nearby. We put a charming, inexpensive kids' mural or picture above the cribs, attached them so the pictures wouldn't move, painted the closets a fun color or used leftover wallpaper, and added a crib to each room. Make sure there is an appropriately placed outlet for the baby monitor. And when used as a nursery, keep the closet door cracked open so air circulates.

Buy the Sink and Cabinet Base in One

You can buy a freestanding cabinet with a sink in it and a granite or soapstone top for far less money than it costs to custom build one; the look is just lovely. I buy Halo cabinets, but there are hundreds online.

Let Them Play

We reinforced two walls in our basement playroom. The kids can throw a baseball, hit a tennis ball, or whack a hockey puck against them. At the opposite end are two basketball nets on top of each other—one for young kids and the other for older kids.

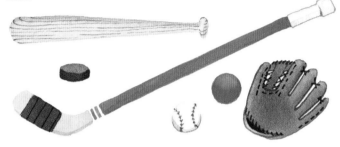

Let There Be Light

We like to "over-light" our home. You can always dim chandeliers or can lights, but having lots of light makes me happy, especially on darker days. It's also nice not to have to deal with tons of lamps. Well-placed lamps make a room warm and wonderful, but if there are too many, your home may look more like a lamp store. You can add maximum light a few ways: look for high-wattage chandeliers or ceiling lights with multiple bulbs and/or add sconces to your walls in key locations. You can add can lights or pin lights to a ceiling as a second source of light.

If you're thinking about using track lighting, keep in mind that it is much easier to add track lights to an existing space (a finished ceiling) than it is to open the ceiling. During a redecorating project, your electrician can usually fish a line to an existing junction box. Frankly I have always hated track lights, but in helping a friend with her home, I found some really interesting ones with antique-style glass bulbs that look fantastic. You can search the Internet for "track lighting heads" and literally, you can find hundreds of styles. And with track lights, you can add as many bulbs as you need to get maximum light.

Under-Amped Light Fixtures

So many light fixtures provide very little light; it is hard to find ones with enough light. Make sure you always ask about the brightness (lumens) of a light bulb, regardless of the technology (halogen, incandescent, CFL, or LED) behind it. A standard 60-watt incandescent bulb, for example, produces about 800 lumens of light. By comparison, a CFL bulb produces that same 800 lumens using fewer than 15 watts. I have had to walk away from so many fixtures as the light level was not anywhere near enough.

Oh-So-Pretty Rain Glass

It is more costly, but rain glass is beautiful for shower doors; you'll have pretty good privacy and you won't see water droplets.

Pocket Doors

I love large open spaces, but pocket doors can be a great way to close off the kitchen so the dog and children are "locked in." Pocket doors can be made for regular-size doors or they can close off large openings like the entryway between the kitchen and the great room. Pocket doors can have wire mesh uppers or be solid wood doors. They can be made of beveled glass, or they can have wood panels. Anything goes. Have fun exploring the options.

Bathroom Storage Options: Closet or Not

Think about building a linen closet into each bedroom or bathroom, or segregating a part of the closet for sheets and towels. You can also plan the space for an armoire, chest, or set of shelves in the bathroom to hold towels, soaps and shampoos, paper products, and more. This is a lovely look and can be much less expensive than a built-in closet.

Round Those Corners

When you are using granite countertops, think about little kids. It is easy in the fabrication process to have the manufacturer soften the corners. It is always a spec on my architect's plans. Then tell the granite supplier again. Squared corners can really hurt.

Newspaper Templates: A Space-Saving Trick

When a room in a newly constructed home is framed, or when I'm redecorating a home, I use newspapers to create a template for furniture so I can check the fit. I literally tape newspaper together (to the exact size of the furniture I am planning to use) and lay the paper on the floor. Then I carry in a few real pieces of furniture to check the three-dimensional fit. For example, I create templates for a chair and a sofa and lay them at the angle I plan to use. Then I place a real chair on top of the "chair template" to see how much space to allow where it meets the corner of the sofa. If I'm planning to add a coffee table, I'll lay down a template for that as well. All too many times, what has looked good on a paper furniture plan does not feel comfortable when the actual furniture is in the room. **Usually the fit is too tight.** Checking in two and three dimensions before purchasing furniture saves lots of aggravation and money.

Consider "Hidden Ovens"

Our family loves to entertain in our kitchens. They're decorated for entertaining. So our ovens and microwaves are low, usually built into the island across from the stove or sink but less visible when looking into the room. It is a little less convenient to cook with lower ovens but truly not too bad at all, and the look is great. If you want your microwave at counter height but don't want to see it, you can hide it behind a cabinet door (this usually requires a deeper cabinet). I put one behind a pretty glass cabinet door with sheers. We went to the trouble of having the doors retract, but frankly most of the time we just leave the cabinet open when the microwave is on, and for dinner parties all is hidden and clean.

The Kitchen Window Box

I love flowers on my windowsill. So, when I was building our new home in Chicago, I told my contractor that I wanted a deep window box that ran the length of the window by the kitchen sink. I asked him to line it in metal so that it didn't leak. I wanted to be able to drop six-inch pots into the box directly from the garden center (four-inch pots would also be fine if the well of the box was built up to accommodate them). It is a luxury, but it's oh so very pretty. It is one of my very favorite looks in my home, and it is so easy to water the plants right in their own planter box. Just a fun thing to do if you are a flower nut like me.

THIS PAGE

A. Glass adds softness

B. Flower box

C. Fancy it up

D. Durable vinyl paper

E. The color of the kitchen changes with the season by changing the painting and the flowers

F. Floor tolerates everything!

G. Hidden ovens

H. Table for five

You Might Want to Add a Refrigerator Later

While you are building, it is easy to add an outlet for a future second refrigerator in the basement or the garage. You may never use it, but adding that outlet during construction doesn't cost much and gives you all the flexibility later. Same goes for a second sink or even a washing machine in the garage. If you think there is a chance you might want it in the future, just add the outlet or pipes now.

Visual Privacy

We redecorated a nice-size two-bedroom apartment in Naples, Florida. There was also a den where we added a pull-out bed, and the den had an adjacent bathroom. We didn't want to close off the room from the main living space with a door, as it wouldn't have looked right, so we added an electric shade that is housed over the door opening in a narrow box that blends well with the room; now the den can serve as a third bedroom. It's not sound-proof, but at least it has good visual privacy.

Doubles over Queens

We had custom bunk beds built—four of them for our lake house. They are made out of logs and can house a whole family, as the beds feature a double mattress above a queen. So incredibly fun.

Plan for Now,
Plan for the Future

....

How many years do you plan to live in your home? Are you fifty-two and building your dream house? **Think NOW about adding an elevator so you will be happy in the home when you are in your eighties.** Even if you put the master bedroom on the first floor, you will still have to get to the other floors. Maybe just think about building the core structurally strong enough to accept an elevator later.

If you don't yet have kids but expect to, plan the house for children now. **You will never have enough storage space.** You want to be able to hide the unbelievable number of toys by easily opening a closet that is off your family room and shoving those toys out of sight. What about play space off your kitchen or family room? Build open play space into the plan if you can, and don't overcrowd it with furniture. Where will the stroller (or two) find a home? You need space for all that crazy kid equipment. Do you have it? Are you decorating for adults? What will happen to that fabric when peanut butter and jelly come for a visit?

Think Handicap

You might want to reinforce the walls in a couple of bathrooms in order to add handicap bars (also called grab bars) later for your parents or a friend who needs them. It is super-cheap to do this when building but is more expensive to install after walls have been built and tiled. And you might want to make one bathroom on the main floor handicap accessible. You never know when you will need it.

Buying Inexpensively

We were building a new home at the lake for our crazy expanding family; we needed a whole bunch of furnishings, and I didn't want to pay a huge sum for them—at least not for the bedrooms, playrooms, and family room. Twice a year in Atlanta there is a furniture and gift trade show. You need to register in advance, but it's not all that hard to gain access. Find a friend with a retail shop, or just about any business can get in. Once you're registered the first time, it is almost an automatic every year thereafter. A trick of the trade that I never knew: many of the furniture showrooms have at least three price discounts and some even four. There is of course the retail price, then the designer price, next the wholesale price, and finally the container or half-container price.

I found this great company that had a showroom; they would make any of their pieces in any color and size, and their prices were reasonable. So, I placed an order for about twenty-two pieces: multiple headboards, bar stools, end tables, bookshelves, coffee tables, and even a kitchen island. Each piece had a one-of-a-kind look that in our rustic lake house would be ideal. We were mixing a lot of these pieces with high-quality pieces made in France and lots of custom millwork, and I was sure the look would be great. When I

returned home, the salesman called me and told me that if I bought four more pieces I could get another twenty pieces free. I was blown away! WHAT? Well, it turned out that if I bought four more pieces, the price would be equal to the half-container pricing. So there is the fourth level. I went to people in my office and explained this deal, and everyone wanted in. It was easy to fill the final twenty pieces, and we brought in a twenty-foot container. The prices for everything were amazing. There are many companies that do this. Look online. Companies like Steven Shell Living, Bima Trading, Bramble, Furniture Classics, and many more price this way. So, if you have a large family or a bunch of friends, **you would be amazed at the discounts you can get if you figure out the game**.

Tricks of the Florist Trade: Making Cut Flowers Last Longer

My thanks to Chris Duquette, a simply GREAT florist, for all he has taught me over the years!

Here are some tips for your cut flowers:

- Make final cuts under running water and cut stems at an angle to increase the surface area for water intake. Try to avoid crushing the stems and place them in water as quickly as possible after cutting. When you cut the stem of a flower, a suction is created—thus the need for an immediate water source. Otherwise air gets up the stem. Also, never use a serrated blade: the cleaner the cut, the better.

- Add a packet of flower preservative to the water if it came with your bouquet, and follow the package directions; it will work better than homemade solutions.

- Remove all leaves that will fall below the water level; it helps enormously by decreasing bacteria.

- Swish bleach around an empty glass vase, pour off the excess (do not rinse out), and then fill with water. It helps keep the water clear.

- To perk up a wilted hydrangea, re-cut the stem and submerge the entire flower completely in water. It will come back to life!

- Add a mist of water daily to keep a steady flow of water and nutrients to the cut flowers. This is especially helpful with hydrangeas, ferns, and foliage.

- Use tepid water for most cut flowers. For tight buds that you want to open quickly, use warm water (no hotter than you can touch safely; if it burns you, it will burn the flowers). Never use frigid or scalding water. Once the blooms are open, use cool water. Putting them in the sun during the opening phase is good, but avoid sunlight when they're in full bloom.

Flower Décor That Lasts

Fresh flowers, especially those cut from your own garden, liven up and add a touch of color and beauty to any room inexpensively. For longer lasting floral arrangements, here are a couple of ideas:

- **Autumn Dried Flower Arrangement:** Dry the flowers and/or foliage of your choice, such as hydrangeas, artichokes, roses, and carnations; hang them upside down in a dry place for a week or so to help them keep their shape (and in some cases even a little more color). Once they are dried, you can further protect them by spraying them with a dry flower sealer, which is available commercially, or even simply with an aerosol hairspray. Start with a dry floral foam block and size it to fit a vase, basket, wood slice, or other container. Insert the flowers and/or foliage into the block. Add succulents for a lovely finish.

- **Holiday Arrangement:** Start with a wet floral foam block and size it to fit a vase, basket, or other container that holds water. Add a variety of items into the foam block that will last an entire month as the "base": consider evergreen sprigs such as spruce, along with other décor that can be attached (use glue or clay) to a stick—such as brightly colored ornament balls, pine cones, and acorns. And then each week you can add flowers and foliage that stay fresh for shorter periods but give your arrangement a burst of color—consider roses, amaryllis, orchids, poinsettia, holly—or attach items like oranges/lemons, limes, cranberries, and apples to a stick and insert into the foam block. Add water to the foam block regularly.

Visit gatherasyougo.com to view holiday arrangements.

Really Good
Silk Flowers

··

There are good silk flowers and very bad silk flowers.
I love real flowers. I can't believe this, but I found
a silk flower place called NDI (ndi.com) that has
some outstanding silk flower arrangements. They
are about the best I've seen, but even some of their
arrangements are better than others. I have some
silk plants in my home with real plants and flowers
in front of them, and no one ever knows they are
not all real. In fact, I had an orchid collection on
my counter in which half were real and half were
fake, and I caught the guy who sells me live orchids
touching each to see which were his!

Family, Family, and More Family...
A Home You Can Live In

OPPOSITE PAGE

A. Vinyl screens that retract in three-seasons room

B. Extra light

C. We *live* in here!

THIS PAGE

A. No plugs on backsplash

B. Half fridge, half pantry

C. Seating for ten

D. Vinyl wipes clean

E. Totally open to the family room

Doors Don't Have to Be Solid

THIS PAGE

A. This door, when fully opened, lays against the wall

B. Baby-safe when closed

Tile and Grout

Our family has a couple of homes, and I like different looks. As an example, one home has a kitchen that is all white, and in another home, the kitchen cabinets are a distressed natural wood tone. As much as I love an all-white kitchen, I would never use white tile on a floor anywhere—not in a kitchen and not in a bathroom. White tile shows everything when used on a floor. And minutes after you have cleaned it, you find hair on it—drives me crazy. You can get an "all-white" kitchen look with any sort of neutral floors, and the contrast of a wood floor with white cabinets is also great.

When you are using tile on horizontal surfaces **never use white grout**. I use DeLorean Gray, which is almost the color of a gray cement. I don't mean barely gray. I mean a gray. It is a color that holds its own against many tiles, regardless of the color, and will look good for decades. I use it with blue Bahia granite tiles, terra-cotta, and all kinds of marble tiles; I have even used it with white wall tile. You can use white grout on vertical white tile as long as you are not splashing spaghetti sauce over it all the time.

Add a Touch of Whimsy!

I love adding a touch of whimsy to a home. Sometimes it's a bronze bear that greets folks near the entry or watches over the pool. Sometimes it's a charming hand-lettered sign that graces a door or is a fun welcome mat for a house. Consider an old-fashioned soda fountain in the recreation room or something as simple as a child's Windsor chair in your family room—even a ferocious alligator is most welcomed on a Florida screened-in porch. Almost anything can add a touch of warmth and help show the personality of the owners. Just have a little fun.

Consider a
Two-Sided Garage

OPPOSITE PAGE

A. Two-sided garage also serves as a party space

THIS PAGE

A. Consider cutting a flower garden into your deck

B. Add blue for contrast

C. Retractable screens

D. Open air for sun

E. Closed to sit outside in the rain

If you budget twenty-dollars per foot for tile...think about a five-dollar-a-foot floor so you have money left for the feature tile.

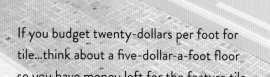
Ⓐ

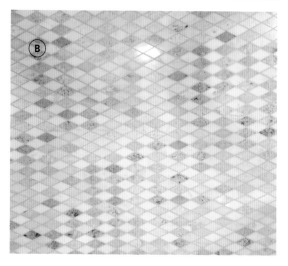
Ⓑ

Low-Cost Flooring Options

THIS PAGE

A. If you budget twenty-dollars per foot for tile... think about a five-dollar-a-foot floor so you have money left for the feature tile.

B. Another version of a low-cost tile

Visit gatherasyougo.com to view a few more design ideas.

With thoughts from

John A. Miller
CEO and President
North American Corporation

My wife, Sandy, and I have known Carol and her family for years and consider them dear friends. Carol and I are also fellow YPO members, and I have had the privilege of serving on the Alberto Culver board. I still serve on the Sally Beauty board.

In every life a little rain will fall...

When we face difficult and challenging times, we often ask, Why me? What could I have done differently to avoid the pain and stress on my friends, family, and self? How do I cope? Where do I go from here?

It's happened to all of us and Carol too. I've heard Carol ask those very same questions through the hardship and loss of a kindred spirit and of family members, through business setbacks and personal disappointments. However, Carol possesses a unique resilience that allows her to reflect deeply, openly share her journey, make a plan, and bounce back. Carol is direct, candid, and forthright about what needs to be done. While she is remarkably kindhearted and embraces the past, Carol always stays focused on the future. Her kids are the true north for all she does—her true passion; that's what helps light the path forward.

I've seen challenging times touch the lives of those in Carol's world, be they family, friends, employees, or even acquaintances. She is always the first to reach out. Without hesitation, Carol offers her hands, resources, experiences, and full heart—all unconditionally. Carol never says no. She's never "half in."

Things Don't Always Go as Planned

My first pregnancy was uneventful until it wasn't. Almost seven weeks before I was due I started bleeding—talk about scary. I was at a restaurant with my husband and friends. We called the doctor, and he said to come to the hospital. My doctor at the time was a cousin of my father-in-law, and the hospital was a local community hospital. Four days after I got there, they decided to check the fluid level surrounding the baby, at which time they realized my water bag had ruptured the night I was admitted. Next thing I knew, I had an emergency C-section. In hindsight, it was four days overdue. But we got lucky. My son was born at four pounds, eleven ounces, and his lungs were well developed. I had a partial rupture of the placenta; the results could have been devastating. But my little boy was healthy, and I was okay too.

A couple of years later we were not so lucky. Again, my pregnancy was uneventful. And again, seven weeks before my due date I was perfectly fine until I experienced unbelievable pain. As luck would have it, we had a meeting at the company with all of our international folks, and I had to excuse myself and could barely walk out the door. I headed to the nurse's office, and she was really concerned. We called my obstetrician, but he was at a family event out of town and couldn't be reached. We then contacted his partner, who was not concerned and told me to go home and rest. I do not like to call doctors, and I seldom complain—but something was crazy wrong with me, and this doctor had told me to go home. Instead, my husband took me to the hospital, and I was barely able to stand the pain. The hospital managed to reach my regular obstetrician, and he called a third partner who rushed over—and once again, I was in for emergency surgery. My placenta had ruptured, and I was bleeding out. My baby boy did not make it, and I was in surgery for several hours. I'm told I was lucky the bleeding was controlled and that the doctor didn't have to do a hysterectomy. It's more than thirty years later, and I still can't describe the devastation of losing that little boy. I was told he was perfect. His name was Matthew.

We found out two weeks later that the doctor who had told me to go home had been diagnosed with a brain tumor a few days after my incident. His partners had known something was not quite right with him, but I guess his actions in my case

There are doctors and there are great doctors. You deserve a really great doctor. If something happens once, it can happen again. Be smarter than I was.

brought it to a head. He died less than a year later. We had all the grounds we needed to sue him and the practice, but what would have been the point? It wouldn't have brought back our baby; and even if we had been advised to go to the hospital sooner, we likely would have lost the baby anyway. It's very scary to know that some doctors will "cover" for other doctors despite grave concerns.

The lessons learned: There are doctors and there are great doctors. You deserve a really great doctor. If something happens once, it can happen again. Be smarter than I was. I liked my obstetrician, and he cared for me a great deal— but he wasn't as good as he should have been. The first time around the doctor and the hospital team should have

confirmed my water bag had broken long before they did, and with the complications of my first pregnancy, they should have been on the lookout for a repeat performance before it happened.

LOOKING FOR NEW DOCTORS

We needed answers. Could I carry another baby to full term or was I destined to only have one child? My family marched me to three high-risk-pregnancy centers in Chicago. One group of experts was sure I had problems with my blood, and they would be taking blood tests every week. Another group was sure I had less capacity than I needed to carry a baby to term, and I would require full bedrest; they hoped that would solve my issues. And the third group, which was the high-risk group at Northwestern Memorial, clearly stated "they just didn't know." The honesty of that approach appealed to me and my family. They told me they would be doing blood work, recommended putting me to bed when I was three or four months pregnant, and hoped to figure it out as I got farther along. There was nothing in my history that had them convinced they had the answers, but their honesty, openness, and lack of hubris was very appealing. I chose Northwestern.

I delivered my son Peter a year after the baby I lost. Peter was seven pounds, and the doctors thought it likely he would have gone to term even if I had not been in bed the last six months. My daughter, Lizzy, was born three years later after another six months of complete bed rest that started immediately after my first trimester. She was born full-term at five pounds. Everyone was pretty convinced that without full bed rest she wouldn't have made it.

It was an incredibly hard lesson to learn: **you never know when you need exceptional care. The smartest docs I know DO NOT have all the answers**. They are constantly open and looking to learn more. They are not afraid to get second opinions—in fact they welcome them. Seek out a teaching hospital and do the research. Find a great doctor.

All Good Doctors Like to Solve Your Problems

My dad is in his late nineties and while he can't walk (spinal stenosis), he is still very sharp, and we all enjoy him a great deal and vice versa. He had a giant career and is used to making things happen. He continually goes to doctors trying to find someone who can make him walk again. Frankly, while sharp as a tack, he has not grown old all that gracefully.

Anyway, one day he complained to his very fine doctor that he just doesn't move his bowels the way he used to (why are older folks so caught up in bowel movements?!?). My aggressive father kept pushing about his bowel movements, and his doctor called me and said he was going to recommend another colonoscopy for my dad. My dad had had one two years earlier, so I pushed back and asked why. He told me of my father complaining, and I asked the doctor what the likelihood was that my father had colon cancer or a bowel blockage; he said probably less than 5 percent—especially because my father was experiencing no pain, bleeding, or other symptoms aside from lack of frequency. So, I told our wonderful doctor that we were going to pass on this latest test. Doctors like to fix problems; it's their job. And this doctor wanted to reassure my dad. But my dad is ninety-seven. Why expose him to the discomfort and relative risk of this test for less than a 5-percent chance?

The lesson here is to **find out what the likelihood is of your having a real problem.** Consider all the circumstances (of course, don't ignore any warning signs) and use your own common sense.

Medicine Withdrawal

I have learned the hard way, seeing Bobby and dear friends go through it: you NEVER stop a medicine cold turkey. Make sure to inform your doctor if you want to stop taking a medication, and research the side effects of withdrawal.

I have a very dear friend who lost her husband, and her doctor suggested an anti-anxiety drug to help her sleep. She took it for a couple of months and decided one day she didn't like feeling tired; so she just stopped taking it. Her symptoms were severe, and she even had to call an ambulance one night and ended up in the emergency room. BE CAREFUL. Check all drugs before you stop taking something. Most of the time you will be told to wean yourself off the medication by adjusting the dosage downward over several weeks or more.

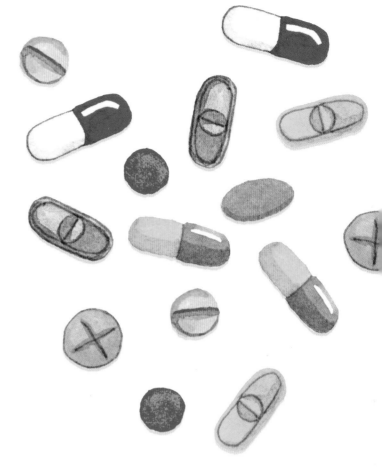

Back Pain and Operations

We recently built our lake house and had a great project supervisor in charge of our job. I saw him every week for eighteen months, and he was always in great shape until one day when he was walking with a crutch. He had done something to his back and was in real pain. He said his doctor was going to give him a steroid shot. I told him that if the doctor told him he needed back surgery, he should call me first. About a month later I got that call; his doctor was recommending immediate surgery because the steroids did not appear to have helped. I suggested that he get a second opinion before he considered surgery. I set him up with doctors at Northwestern Memorial Hospital. He called later and thanked me. The doctors had told him there was NO WAY surgery should be done at that point. Insurance would pay for physical therapy and cortisone shots, and that's what they recommended he try before he even thought about surgery. Six weeks later he showed up at my house without a crutch and without pain.

Be careful, folks; get the second opinion. And if the second opinion is in opposition to the first one, then get a third opinion. The goal is to find two reputable sources whose opinions are in agreement. There are more ways than one to treat almost any issue, and you will find that the way physicians treat a given illness or injury is updated all the time. But, of course, there are times when immediate care is needed, including surgery. Never neglect an emergency.

When a Friend Is Feeling Low

Here's a lovely gift idea. Friends gave this to me when I was going through a difficult time.

1. Get a glass jar, a basket, or any pretty and fun container.
2. Give five friends (or more) ten small colored strips of paper (uniform in size) each and have them fill out all ten strips with a special memory or saying—something that is important or will bring a smile to your friend who is feeling low.
3. Fold and place the strips of paper in the container.
4. Give this gift of the heart to your friend with instructions to read one anytime he or she needs to be reminded how much they are loved.

Kind and loving gestures help.

Anger in the House

I have a very dear friend. He is a super dad with a couple of kids, each very different. One child is smart and a great athlete, while the other has significant learning disabilities. His kids are great.

Many years ago, he was always coaching his one son's soccer team. And when a parent had a concern about their kid, he would handle it diplomatically. But he would also be tough. He would listen, share rules and requirements, and also find gentle ways to help address the concern. He was always advocating for the kids on his team in a positive way.

With his wife, on the other hand, he was always finding lots of problems—lots and lots of problems. He would complain to me about her. I am pretty sure he was complaining to her as well.

Set a Date in the Future

When I am grieving, when I am getting over an operation, or when something has really upset me, **I try to set a date in my mind** by which it's plausible that life will be better. For instance: I had two torn menisci, and I had both knees operated on at the same time. It was May. I was not happy. I set a date in my mind three months from the operation and kept telling myself to focus on that date: that by the end of August I would be pain-free and happy. It helped to get past the "here and now." It's also a good thing to do when your newborn has you completely sleep-deprived or when your five-year-old has a broken leg in a cast and is driving you nuts. Set a date in the not-too-distant future, and look forward to it. If it's feasible, plan something you will enjoy doing, from a simple walk on the beach to a major project or even a vacation. Having a goal will make the wait more bearable and possibly more productive.

He thought her upbringing was the cause of her problems: the way she handled the kids was wrong, she didn't seem satisfied with how much money he made—just a whole bunch of issues. I said to him one day, "Gosh, if another coach was complaining about the kids on your soccer team the way you complain about your wife (all the time), you would hand that coach his head. You have to figure this out. Either get out of the marriage or fix it. She is one of yours, just like your kids."

He loved his wife, and the light went on. I just may have helped that marriage a lot. Everyone has problems with their marriage, but when it is a constant barrage, you have to take a look at yourself and maybe think of getting out, or just maybe you need to change your attitude. I heard Susan St. James say one time, **"Anger is like taking poison and hoping the other person will die."** That's a really powerful statement.

The fact is that dying with as much grace as we can muster is the last lesson we can teach our children — and it's a huge lesson.

Facing the Worst— and How You Handle It

I had two friends. Both of them were diagnosed with cancer within a year of each other. One dear friend had ovarian cancer. She would never be cancer-free regardless of what treatments occurred. She had a great husband and five children, the oldest in college and the youngest in grade school. My other friend was diagnosed with stage-four liver cancer. She was also married and had two children, the youngest in his teens. Both of these diagnoses offered very little hope. I was pretty darn close to these women, both of whom were only in their early forties.

The huge lesson for me was how differently my friends handled the next years of their lives. One was positive all the time. She was very Catholic and her whole approach to all of this was, "Why not me?" Maybe it was her faith that made her so positive, but she was an outstanding example for all of us. She managed to live for about seven years with ovarian cancer, which is in itself a miracle. No matter when you saw her, regardless of the treatment effects, she was wonderful to be with and a glowing example. My other friend was

very difficult to be with. Of course, she was going through the worst life has to offer, but she couldn't find the strength to be positive about anything. She wasn't terrible—just always upset and always dwelling on the inevitable. She spent the couple years she had left pretty much in the dumps. They were both good people. But the fact is it was so much easier to be with one friend than the other. As a result, people spent more time with the friend who tried to be a positive example.

Bobby and I talked about this a lot. We knew his time was limited. The fact is that dying with as much grace as we can muster is the last lesson we can teach our children—and it's a huge lesson. It's so hard to find your strength and be positive in a situation that is very difficult. But be positive if you can. Another friend recently lost her husband, and I was deeply moved by her note to me. She said, "He taught me how to live, and he certainly taught me how to die." It still gives me chills as I write this. Thanks for sharing that, Mimi.

Kind Remembrances

After someone you care about passes away, of course you can send a donation to the charity they designated or flowers to the funeral home. Another very kind remembrance is to send a gift to the grandkids—or money to add to a college fund—or something the family wouldn't buy for themselves but that is a gift from you in honor of their loved one. A garden bench with an engraved plaque could be purchased for a park or university, or could be for their own backyard. Even a restaurant gift card for a family dinner out to celebrate their loved one is a wonderful and welcome gift.

When People Pass Away

Bobby died at home; it was the only thing left that I could do for him. Thankfully he wasn't in pain. Brain cancer is awful. It takes so much of you, but it is not painful. He was strong and courageous right up to the very end.

Bob had so many friends. He was a great golfer and had run several large companies. And I have a whole lot of friends and people who care about me and my family. So the memorial service was large, personal, and pretty special. But what totally surprised me was how many people I hardly knew who reached out to me with real kindness. Funny thing to say, but I have to "up my game" when other folks pass away. I had thought it would be intrusive to send notes to folks I had met only a few times. I didn't want to bother people in their time of sorrow. But after Bobby's passing, I now realize it is fine and good to reach out to just about anyone if their passing touches you in some way. I think I am a pretty emotionally intelligent person, but I missed this one. Telling people you care is always the right thing to do.

Think a Little Outside the Norm When People Pass Away

If the person who passed meant a lot to you, or to someone you know well, consider doing something special a few weeks later. There is often an outpouring of love and attention in the days after a loved one dies. But as too many of us know, the loneliness is worse as the weeks progress.

Here are a few ideas:

- Send a letter with special memories of the person who passed.
- Arrange a visit with loved ones...share stories and listen to their stories.
- Frame a special photo of their loved one.
- Prepare meals in containers that don't need to be returned; include instructions for cooking, reheating, or freezing.
- Deliver a giant stuffed bear holding a bottle of wine.
- Arrange an experience that you can do together and share the simple pleasures of life and friendship: ride bikes, walk on the beach, or see a movie.
- Send two tickets to a sporting event, concert, or show that you will attend with them two months later.
- Deliver a tabletop Christmas tree pre-lit and decorated with "photo ornaments" of the person who passed with family and friends.
- And if it is welcomed...bring a puppy to love with all the necessities (crate, food, toys, food/water dish, etc.)...but by all means, ask first!

CHAPTER 05

Celebrations

evening as they stagger out weighed down by bags of toys and huge inflatables to take home, you know you've been part of a wild and unique experience. (Good news: all this "junk" was underwritten.)

So, whether you are decorating for a junior high school graduation party or a world-class charity event, if the theme is important, stop early on and think about what works to convey the theme. Can you think of dozens of ways to visualize what you want to show? An outer-space theme is way more difficult than Beach, Diamonds and Denim (cowboys, horses, western, or anything glitzy), or Remember When (where anything nostalgic works, from a penny candy display to old-time TV posters). Think of the music you can add to enhance the themes. This is all so incredibly broad that wherever your imagination takes you, you'll have to narrow it down rather than bulk it up. The Birthday Bash gives you the opportunity to decorate with hundreds of wrapped packages—filled or not filled. Dessert can be birthday cakes, and favor bags are treats from yo-yos to bubbles. (Careful of bubbles getting on the ladies' gowns.) The party display can be red wagons, dolls, and teddy bears all dressed for a party. One of my favorite themes was Boys and Their Toys. Centerpieces were metal cars—red and black Ferraris. We

had every classy boy toy woven into all of our décor. Items are cheaper and more plentiful for all of these themes than they are for Outer Space or Around the World.

Easy Themes:

- Toyland
- Ladies' Day at the Lake
- Garden Party
- Party in Pink
- The Summer Ball
- A Day at the Fair
- The Birthday Ball
- The Red, Black, and White Ball (or pick the colors of your favorite sports team)
- The Circus, The Circus
- Cartoon Land
- Bedazzled: anything and everything glitzy
- The Holiday Ball
- America: American food, colleges, sports, holidays, music, red-white-and-blue decorations and garb
- Tailgate: colleges only
- Remember When: old movies, toys, candy, cartoons, TV shows
- Under the Sea
- Las Vegas or New Orleans
- Candyland
- Beach: all kinds of ways to take this, from inflatables to carnival stuffed fish
- Christmas anything: caroling, cookie baking, gingerbread house making, cookie exchange, ornament exchange
- Any kind of costume party, and tie it to an era like the 1970s or even a pajama party
- The Locker Room: any and all toys, games, sporting equipment
- Black and White: everyone dresses in black and white and all décor and favors are black and white; include silver metallic to add the glitz

Stop early on and think about what works to convey the theme.

Baby and Wedding Showers

Our invitations say gifts are to be "unwrapped pretty." That translates to "show the gift you are giving." Put it in a basket or a box and leave the box open. Decorate the outside of the box with beautiful ribbons. We set up pretty tables where the gifts are displayed. It makes the room's "look," guests love seeing all the presents, and no one has to sit and watch the new mom or the bride open tons of gifts.

If you are the hostess, a couple of tips for your "unwrapped pretty" display table:

- Use tablecloths that add to the party's theme and color.
- Set out about fifteen four-inch colorful blooming plants to add color to your display.
- Have one or two people ready to help you accept the gifts from guests as they arrive.
- Keep a list of who brought what in case the card gets separated.
- Supply some little cards in case a guest or two forgot to add their name to their gift.

- Open each person's card and tape it on the gift. Guests like to see who gave or sent what.
- Have a supply of extra-large bows ready to go in case some gifts arrive undecorated or you need to unwrap a few.
- Make your gift a centerpiece; think about what you can give to add to the look of the décor on the gift table.
- Take photos of the display for the honoree.

"Unwrapped Pretty"

PLEASE BRING YOUR GIFT WITHOUT PAPER OR BAG
SIMPLY USE A BOW AND A GIFT TAG.
AN UNWRAPPED PRESENT IS JUST AS SWEET
AND WILL SAVE MORE TIME TO MINGLE AND EAT.
WE'LL DISPLAY YOUR GIFTS FOR ALL TO SEE,
THEN RELAX AND HONOR THE MOM-TO-BE!

Instead of a Sit-Down Luncheon...Something Special for a Wedding Shower

It's fun to find ways to make showers extra special for the bride, and for her guests too.

A few ideas:

- Do a cooking shower where you have a chef teach your guests how to cook something unusual and interesting or teach the tricks of great display: the ultimate cheese tray, edible flowers, the best-looking and easiest watermelon basket ever.
- Have a creative shower at which you teach the guests how to arrange flowers in one room and how to create or wrap magical packages in another.
- Host a bar shower at a local restaurant for guys and gals. Have the bartender show everyone how to make fantastic concoctions. Bring in live music and party on.
- Rent a bowling alley and serve bar food. Supply cowboy hats.
- Consider a beach bridal party or an old-fashioned cookout.
- Which friend has an incredible garden you can borrow for an outdoor ladies' day?
- Rent a boat and do a wedding shower cruise.
- Hold a tailgate party for big football fans.
- Frankly, any party idea you can think of can be done for the bride or for the bride and groom. Get creative—it will make the day more special for all.

About Those Wedding Gifts

No new news here...but the world has changed. Some young couples live together for years before they tie the knot and have already accumulated most of the home necessities. And many are passing on fine china, crystal, and sterling. We've enjoyed giving other types of gifts, especially those that include an "experience," which I know most young people love. Almost anything works!

Here are some fun gifts we have given to celebrate the bride and groom:

- A tree in their yard
- An outdoor grill
- A gasoline gift card
- One-year anniversary dinner set up at a favorite restaurant
- Skis or snowshoes
- A special dinner on their honeymoon
- Preloaded Visa cards
- Mountain bikes
- Cases of wine
- Camping equipment
- Airline gift cards to help bring family in for the wedding or cover travel to a honeymoon destination
- Blue Apron or some other home delivery service that provides easy-to-prepare meals
- Cooking lessons for two
- A basket of garden tools and several hundred tulip bulbs (for those who love gardening)
- A weekend getaway to a romantic destination
- Matching luggage
- Chef for a home dinner party
- Whole Foods gift card

these little surprises were unwrapped and just cute, not so much fantastic gifts as just silly fun. Gifts were anything from mini bags of candy to ice cream scoops with charming handles, pretty decks of cards, stationery, a candle, a mini frame, or a bottle of perfume. It was so comical to see people chase down the pocket ladies. Everyone loves surprises.

And we had a **cake walk**. A cake walk is described in detail below in case you have never danced for a cake before.

And at the end of the day, we had **cocktails and a boat ride** that took us on a forty-minute tour of so many of the pretty homes along Lake Geneva. Crazy day I know, but so fun to celebrate the women in my life who are always doing so much for others. I loved planning it. It made me think happy thoughts at a tough time in my life, and everyone had a ball.

Cake Walk at the Lake
During my childhood, one of my favorite school carnival games was the cake walk. A cake walk is sort of like musical chairs without the chairs. Anywhere from ten to twenty squares (depending on the number of guests and the size of the room) are marked off on the floor with tape, and each square has a number on it; consider adding numbers to hockey pucks or other comparable items. While a fun music track (or band) is playing, the guests "dance" from square to square. When the music stops, the dancers stand still in the square on which they landed, and a number is drawn from a hatful of numbers corresponding to the squares on the floor. The guest whose number is called gets the cake of his or her choice. As the game progresses, the number of squares on the floor is reduced (by simply removing the hockey pucks), and the corresponding numbers are removed from the hat.

We "upped" this concept at the "Ladies' Day at the Lake" party. I bought Bundt cakes, coffee cakes, cupcakes, and eclairs and wrapped them in crinkly cellophane paper. We ordered oversize jars of cookies and had twenty mini cakes and a few large ones all displayed on the oversize island in our

kitchen. The look was beyond charming. I bought inexpensive platters and cake plates, or just simple dinner plates (Home Goods!), and those were part of the gift. EVERYONE wanted to play. We ended when we ran out of cakes, but the whole thing was just a hoot.

Consider doing a Christmas cookie walk, for which all your guests bring cookies and you display them as the prizes. You can also have guests bring cakes, desserts, or other sweets. It's a creative way to have everyone take home a "favor" that they supplied themselves or, for not too much money, you can supply the treats yourself. If you're planning a garden party, you can create the same concept with potted plants. It's a great way to get people moving, and the competitive nature of your guests will result in lots of laughs.

Witches' Ball

Every other year I host the Witches' Ball, for women only, and it is WILD! The women come dressed in their finest witch attire. I mix lawyers, CEOs, teachers, stay-at-home moms, and women my mother's age—along with women who work with me: my housekeeper and the nurses who care for my dad. All these fun and crazy women dress to the nines. My daughter and daughters-in-law are invited to come and bring a couple of friends, so we have ten to fifteen women who are in their early thirties; but most of the women are between forty-five and seventy-five. It is held at the "bar of the frog," which, of course, is Hugo's Frog Bar in Chicago. We hire a great disc jockey, a magician who roams the tables, and a couple of great-looking actors (males only) who dress in costume and dance with the hundred-plus women all night long. We pass out a bunch of favors throughout the night including flashing lights, and green or scarlet cocktails are served in light-up glasses. Treasures abound and it is all just plain crazy. The music never stops, nor does the dancing. I think when women dress up and can just play, it is the most fun thing to watch and to be a part of. The pictures tell the story.

A Party in Pink

Pink is hot! Use it for a sweet-sixteen birthday, a baby shower, a sixty-fifth birthday, or just about any celebration.

Consider using some or all of these:
- Pink candies (M&Ms, pink-wrapped Hershey's Kisses, pink candy necklaces)
- Pink flowers
- Pink linens
- Pink favors (pink bead necklaces, pink enamel frames, sun hats in pink, pink baby bottles, pink purses, pink wallets, pink pashminas or scarves, pink stationery or pencils, pink travel bags with embroidered initials, pink nail polish, any pretty outer box in pink with anything inside)

For food:
- Pink cupcakes
- Pink macaroons
- Pink ice cream or sorbet
- Pink lemonade
- Frozen strawberry daiquiris
- Huge pink candy ribbon suckers
- Pink sugar cookies
- Pink gumballs

Add some white teddy bears dressed in pink T-shirts. We could go on for pages. This idea can work for just about any color—a friend's favorite blue, a bride's wedding colors, a guy's golf-theme party (think green!). The consistent use of a single color is delightful.

Celebration of Life Events

A wonderful way to make a celebration of life warmer is to give each guest a small potted plant to take home. Use the plants as décor for the event; even four-inch pots will do. Invite your guests to take one with them as they leave. You can include a little hang tag on each pot that thanks the guests for bringing joy to your family and invites them to think about your loved one and all the special times they shared, as they nurture this little plant for years.

The Company Party: Décor to Give Away

At the Alberto Christmas black-tie event that we held for our employees and customers every year, we had a huge budget for flowers. I was in charge of the décor for this party for a number of years. And after seeing those thousands of dollars spent on flowers that lasted for only a night or two, we changed our thinking and made magic happen for local charities and our guests. Each year we looked for a special favor that would go home with our guests, and we made these the key element of our centerpieces and room décor. The look was charming. Some years the giveaways were porcelain dolls in Christmas dress, huge golden reindeer, or giant trains carrying candy. One year we contracted for someone to make mini candy houses and each guest received one. Another year everyone walked out with a three-foot bear and another year with a waist-high,

fully decorated mini tree. We would place all the themed giveaways around the various rooms and they made the space so festive. At dinner, everyone chose a tiny box (with a single chocolate candy in each) that had a number on the bottom. The number corresponded to a giveaway. Everyone loved it (almost too much, as the RSVP rate kept increasing).

Even more rewarding, the ballroom and cocktail reception areas were decorated with twenty-five full-size Christmas trees. Each tree had a glittering banner naming the charitable organization to which the tree was going to be delivered the next day, and each tree had about eighty small gifts tied on it. The gifts matched the décor of the party and each year looked somewhat different. Trees would have everything from stuffed toys wired to their branches, to cars, books, games, and dolls. Each tree also had mittens and hats mixed in with the toys. The trees were lighted and magical. The guests felt great about the outpouring of generosity, our people felt proud, and our maintenance men who delivered the trees the next day claimed it was one of the most rewarding things

Each tree had a glittering banner naming the CHARITABLE ORGANIZATION to which the tree was going to be delivered the next day.

they did each year. And guess what? We spent less than in earlier years trying to make a couple of huge ballrooms look great with flowers. Obviously, this can be done for charity balls as well. We've done it with birch trees in the middle of summer, and we fully decorated a ballroom with summertime inflatables that were later given to summer camps for underprivileged kids.

Fabulous Favors for a Fiftieth Anniversary Party

We had a black-tie dinner party for my parents' fiftieth wedding anniversary. My mom loved all kinds of flowers, and she loved to share her love of flowers. She had a greenhouse and would spend hours "up there" teaching anyone who would listen. For their party, we decorated a large room with beautiful china pots of blooming plants—each more lovely than the next. We always give a party favor at each of our events, and this time, we gave the guests wonderful flowers that would bloom for months and serve as a tribute to my mom. The fact that the plants saved us money on décor was a bonus.

Getting to Know You

So you are new in town. You know a few wonderful people already, but you want to get to know a few more people, some of whom you hope can become really good friends. Invite the people you know to come to a luncheon or cocktail party at your home and ask each guest to bring two friends who would be fun for you to get to know. Entertaining in your home lets people know the real you. Dazzle them with your cooking expertise or simply set a pretty table and order in. Keep it simple and relaxed.

And when you have a friend who has recently moved to town, offer to host the same kind of event for him or her—at your place or theirs. It's a fun and very kind thing to do.

Let Your Guests Help Plan the Fun

We love to have friends come and visit or travel with us. And I love to put them to work. To make the time more exciting for all (and less work for me), I ask people to plan an evening or an event. Our friends really get into it.

We had a group of twenty people come to our horse farm in Ocala, Florida, for a long weekend. I divided the group into teams and gave them the rules of engagement. I always plan big breakfasts and at least one major evening meal, but the other nights and lunches I leave up to my friends to plan. When they're invited to be 100 percent our guests, I will set a budget and distribute the dollars to the team leader. I would have spent this money anyway—I just make it more interesting by having my friends do the planning. When we are going somewhere Dutch treat, we all put the same amount of money into the pot, divide it up, and let the games begin. At the farm, my event was a western-style barbecue. People dressed up, and I provided cowboy hats and brought in a dancer to teach us all line dancing under the stars (on our driveway). The grill was set on the pavement; the meat cooking outdoors smelled fantastic, the horses were at the fence line, and the dogs were running around crazy excited. Country music blared from the iPod, and libations were colorful. Such incredible fun. We all ended up in the pool after a bonfire and songs.

That same weekend my friends planned a tailgate party, and everyone was invited to wear their college gear. Of course, we had beer and bag-toss games, a tape of music from our college days, a pickup truck with bales of hay, Frisbee games, and touch football. It was so clever.

Except for a couple of hints to help our friends pack, all these events are kept secret until the "night of," with a teaser invitation delivered to the guests when they arrive. The third night people were invited to wear white, and it was a *Great Gatsby*–style party with champagne, croquet, jazz, and a more formal dinner.

When you share the planning, people get competitive and creative, and the weekend is just more fun. On another occasion, we had friends join us in Las Vegas. We arranged for Elvis to appear, and my friends were the "Sweet Potato Queens" (that was something to see: two of these ladies were propositioned on the assumption they were ladies of the evening. Uh oh.). I have been a part of treasure hunts, a kids'-style birthday party for big folks, beach parties, murder mysteries, music fests, costume parties, parties that celebrated the Seventies, Hollywood glamour, war games (paintball tournaments), and so much more.

Share the work, Share the fun.

Be creative!

What's Cooking?
Come & Enjoy
As We Shower
Haley O'Brien
With Food, Fun &
A Few Tricks In The Kitchen

The Chopping Block
Merchandise Mart Plaza
Suite 107 – Chicago
Enter On W. Kinzie Street

Sunday Brunch
May 15th ♥ 10am

Given by: Carol Bernick,
Madelon Gryll & Marty Whealy

Haley Is Registered At
Bed Bath & Beyond, Crate & Barrel
& Williams Sonoma

It's An Entertaining Shower...
Please Bring Gifts Unwrapped Pretty

Kindly Reply: 312.477.7601
kanderson@polishednickelcapital.com

Join us if you Dare...
You're in for a Scare!
Fly, Creep or Crawl to our
Witches' Ball
Thursday October 27

Tablecloths Are Key

For just about any event, you can add
real punch and power to your décor
with a cloth in a great color. My advice
is to spend the money on great-looking
cloths because you can get away with
much less décor if the cloth makes a
statement. You can rent them. But if
you buy or make them, then they can
be repurposed for many more parties in
the future.

All About Candy

Candy is a colorful, easy treat with which to decorate almost anything. I have used it in so many ways. People enjoy candy no matter if it's the finest chocolate or penny candy. Think about using candy to:

- Make a wreath, an ornament, or a gum-drop tree.
- Build a candy train or a chain for a Christmas tree.
- Serve as a nametag or a place card.
- Decorate donuts, cupcakes, candy houses, cookies, ice cream, birthday cakes.
- Brighten up a wedding, a black-tie event, a charity party, or a child's birthday.
- Concentrate the colors for a fantastic look, using three shades of greens or six kinds of candy in shiny silver.
- Add multiple colors—the variety says HAPPY.
- Make a candy necklace out of wrapped candy—simply string it on ribbon.
- Fill interesting shaped bottles, sprinkle candy over a tablecloth, layer on a surface, or spell out words.
- Include in a party invitation—or make it the invitation.
- Serve as a party favor or gift (try filling cellophane bags or a giant jar!).
- Place something as simple as Nerds or M&M's on a white table cloth—it makes a silly and fun presentation.
- Customize a gift: for example, make a photo wrapper to cover a chocolate bar.
- Use as a wedding favor: oversize chocolate turtles or cello bags of Hershey's Kisses.
- Set out in bowls, bags, or boxes.
- Make a basket of someone's favorites—it's a welcome gift almost any time.

I could go on and on. Search Google for "candy as a decoration" or search a color of the candy you want to use. Look at Candy.com, candywarehouse.com, or any of a dozen other great sites online. Have fun! Enjoy. At the 2017 Oscars: candy came floating down on mini parachutes, and the crowd went wild. Just about anything with candy works. Yay for Willy Wonka!

Creating Décor that Is Simple, Lovely, and Cheap

When you have a party or when you decorate your home, the décor can be simple, lovely, and inexpensive. Check out these photographs.

More Simple Décor

Love with your whole Heart♡Cherish Family♡Have Faith♡Give Thanks♡

Lindsey and Craig

Getting Hitched♡February 11, 2012

Hold Hands♡Celebrate Friends♡Dream Big♡Light a Candle

Nickel & Nickel

& Nickel

On Buying Cheap for Parties and More

I like a deal as much as anyone. In fact, I bet I like a deal more than most. I visit a closeout show in Las Vegas every year where I have bought, at huge discounts, items for charities I am in charge of, corporate gifts for all our employees, and any and every party favor I have ever needed for the smallest crew at a child's birthday party to a benefit for a thousand folks.

If you are interested, the show is called ASD Market Week. If you plan on going, you can't see half of the show in three full days. But be ready: it is like one giant flea market—maybe a bit better than that, but not much. Having said that, when I get all this stuff opened and displayed, no one realizes it is closeout merchandise and I have often paid 50 to 80 percent off the wholesale prices. Just wear your walking shoes. Jeans are fine.

I have bought everything from television sets to small appliances, toys, anything for the home, wrapping paper, clothing, and collectibles. Just about anything you can think of, you can find. There are also jewelry, gift, and fashion shows (and sometimes the great furniture show, too) that run at the same time. These shows are wholesale, not closeouts, but are incredibly worthwhile. It doesn't take much to get into these shows, but you do need to register in advance. Most business cards will qualify you.

It's a fun show to go to with a couple of friends, and you can often split the case packs. If you are buying for a school or charity, this show is a must. One caution that I have learned over the years is that some things don't last forever: avoid clay and markers, check out the stickiness of the stickers you might find, and avoid closeout food.

If you decide to go, a couple of "terms of the trade" will be helpful:

- What is your minimum? (How much do you have to buy to place an order?) Sometimes the minimum is way more than you want to spend, and sometimes it is a case pack, which can be as few as twelve of the same thing.
- What is your lead time? (How long until you will receive the merchandise?)
- From where are you shipping? (That helps you estimate shipping costs—the closer the cheaper.)
- What is the seller's policy if something arrives broken? Seems simple but some of these companies are big and have been in the closeout business for decades; some are not as reputable. Listen to their commentary and see if they appear to be a quality source. Keep in mind that you are buying closeouts so you don't always get 100 percent of what you order; but the prices are incredibly worth it. And don't forget to bargain, especially if you are buying a lot or go on the last day.

Photograph the Look and Record the Data

I found myself doing the same things over and over. Every time I planned a dinner party, I would pull out all my stuff to figure out how many people I could serve without having to rent anything, what plates looked good with what linens, and if I used all those dinner plates, did I have enough china for dessert as well. We entertain a lot, and sometimes that means a sit-down dinner for thirty or forty people or a buffet for a couple hundred. **I now take pictures of everything—literally, a close-up of a place setting with the silverware, dishes, linens, glasses, even down to the salt shakers.** I do the same for large buffets or for my Labor Day barbecue. Also key is capturing where I put all those tables and what furniture I had to move. I keep all this in a simple binder (easier to flip through) and on my computer as well. Over the years, I have had bunches of events, and I can easily pull an evening together and have it look fantastic by recycling really good ideas. Of course, I mix it up and add new touches to each event—that makes it special—but having captured all my past thinking and "looks" sure makes life easier.

Take key photos of your Christmas décor (or Halloween or any other occasion for which you decorate) to help you remember what goes where. I have way too much stuff I love and people keep bringing my family more holiday treasures. I photograph the house, and again I have a simple binder that I can refer to when I'm ready to set out all these items without having to figure out placement all over again. Saves time for more celebrating.

All About Weddings

We went to eight weddings in one summer, each one prettier than the last. Having said that, at many of them we were looking at our watches waiting for the evening to end. Knowing that we had a couple of weddings in our family in the next year (it turned out to be three in the next nine months!), we took a hard look at what we were planning and made a family pledge to make these weddings really FUN for our family and guests. Once we made that decision, our planning changed. And based on the fact that we had to turn off the lights at the end of the evening and send many people home, we believe we succeeded.

Here are a few suggestions to increase the fun:

- Limit the wedding-night speeches to two people and try hard to hold them to less than five minutes; all the rest of the speeches could be given at the rehearsal dinner with a more intimate crowd.

- Offer a few "special drinks" in miniature glasses, creating the "Ooh, what's that?" effect at cocktail receptions. Or decorate your drinks: think about how much more inviting a drink is when it has a lovely, juicy strawberry, a slice of lime, or a chunk of fresh pineapple on the rim of the glass. Even a colored straw or a stirrer can carry the initials of the bride and groom and make everything more festive.

- Have guests walk in to music so that dancing begins as the doors to the ballroom open. At so many wedding receptions the night is half over before the dance music begins. It sets an uplifting mood to "rock out" as you enter.

- Pass mini milkshakes, black cows, ice cream sundaes, and even mini banana splits. Try mini cups of gelato, mini bags of French fries, or sliders. Just about anything can be made in miniature, and people enjoy eating miniatures of almost any kind.

- Offer great-looking dessert buffets. You can feature foods from a particular area of the country where your bride or groom are from. For example: Georgia—peach cobbler, Florida—Key lime pie.

- Serve the bride or groom's favorite dessert, be it banana pudding or apple pie. If they love chocolate, an entire chocolate room can be enticing. The obvious start is a great chocolate cake surrounded by mini cupcakes; but also think of chocolate-covered pretzels; chocolate-covered fruits, nuts, and marshmallows; five kinds of chocolate ice cream, giant chocolate-covered turtles, chocolate milk shakes, and malts. Make it super fun and memorable. It can be elegant, glorious, and fun all the same time.

- Feature a candy display, glamorous or whimsical, all one color or in a mixture of colors. Or you might have a server offer selections of gourmet candies from an assortment; provide mini candy boxes and invite guests to choose four truffles from a fabulous display case. Invite guests to take home an assortment of homemade treats, in a custom box of course. For the few who don't love chocolate, have waiters pass mini cheesecakes or fruit and sorbet in small waffle-cone baskets.

- Spend a little bit less on the meal and more on the fun pass-outs that happen later in the evening to move from a lovely wedding to a GREAT exciting party. Or you can fill buckets with takeaways: think sunglasses, boas, hats of all kinds (cowboy hats, straw hats, flashing glitter hats, baseball caps either themed to the location of the wedding or with the logo of your favorite sports team or college—or create a logo themed to the wedding), light-ups, jewels, flasks, custom T-shirts, cigars (chocolate candy or the real thing), pashminas, and hundreds more. Just take your theme or colors and run with it. If your wedding color is purple, have fun with purple. If it's gold and white, go a little crazy with gold and white. People love to be treated as kids, and everyone loves (good-quality) free stuff.

Wedding Trifecta

LET THE WONDER NEVER CEASE!

Lizzy and Dan
Lake Geneva
July 16, 2011

Lindsey and Craig
Chicago
February 11, 2012

Barbara and Peter
Bahamas
April 28, 2012

PEACE ON EARTH BEGINS AT HOME

Our family Christmas card for 2012.

Three Weddings in Nine Months

My children are all three and a half years apart. Due to my high-risk pregnancies, this translates to my oldest being seven years older than my youngest. Yet all my darling children decided to get married at virtually the same time. Are you kidding me? Planning and executing all three weddings in such a short time, and trying hard to make each one incredibly special and different from the others, was one of the harder things I have done in my life.

My daughter Lizzy's wedding to Dan came first, and she is the youngest. My middle son, Peter, and his fiancée, Barbara, planned an April destination wedding in the Bahamas; Barb's mom died when she was young so it was our pleasure to plan that wedding. And my oldest son, Craig, and his fiancée, Lindsey, jumped in between. Lindsey's mom had recently lost her husband and we stepped in to plan and help. So three for three—what nicer gift could I give my kids?

If your children are like mine, they want to know everything that's happening with the wedding planning. Frankly, they were pretty easy to deal with and were grateful for all the efforts that went into three weddings so close together. But the weddings were theirs, after all, and they liked to know what their crazy mom was up to. They chose colors, the venue, and clothing and had input on almost everything—but I still hold that it is super fun to have a couple of things the wedding couple doesn't know about; so in each of the wedding sections you will hear about all the surprises we planned.

What follows is not a picture album of our family, but pictures of décor, signage, special events, and more. Feel free to copy anything or take an idea or two from what follows.

Lizzy and Dan

JULY, IN LAKE GENEVA, WISCONSIN

The theme of my daughter's wedding was "a taste of New Orleans meets Old Wisconsin," crazy as that sounds. Lizzy went to Tulane and fell in love with New Orleans (NOLA), and her husband was a true Midwesterner, so we wanted to feature foods from NOLA and from Wisconsin—the site of the wedding ceremony and reception. Appetizers included fried oysters and crawfish étouffée as well as mini brats and soft pretzels with cheese—all elegantly served. Dessert was truly terrific with stations that served bananas Foster—a NOLA favorite—and fruit cobblers with homemade ice cream, a Wisconsin treat. The most fun were the very famous Doberge cakes, all fourteen of them, that we had sent from New Orleans. They were fantastic and were gone early in the evening.

The Rehearsal Dinner: the Geneva Inn (a country inn)
The Meet-and-Greet for anyone coming to town: around the fire pit at the Abbey Resort in Lake Geneva
The Wedding and Dinner Reception: Welcome Home (the name of our Wisconsin home)
The After Party: Old New Orleans—celebrating jazz and Mardi Gras at the Abbey
The Day-After Brunch: given by friends—a farmer's market theme

LIZ & DAN
COCKTAILS
DANCING
LAKE
GOOD FOOD

SPECIAL SURPRISES FOR LIZZY AND DAN

- We made a "tree of blessings" with a lovely clump hawthorn that would later be planted in our yard. Under the tree we had a charming green-and-white wooden dollhouse with a "mail slot" cut into the roof. Our guests were encouraged to write a message or a blessing to our kids and drop it in the dollhouse. Next to the house were two child-size Adirondack chairs (indicating someday there may be little ones). The tree was lit with miniature white lights and was a lovely display at the entrance to the reception tent. If a tree is more than you can plant, a rose bush works well too.

- Dan loves cookies. We had a huge cookie display with a large, wonderful sign that said "Cookies for Dan and All His Friends." We offered at least thirty kinds of cookies in charming bags tied in green and white. Our guests took home a jar full of mini cookies as a wedding favor. Each had a label on it, in green and white of course, with charming sayings about love and marriage, plus the date and location of the wedding. Little bags of cookies were available to sample as part of the dessert buffet.

- A note on the cookie display: it was precious, but if you can get away with a candy display, it will be easier! Cookies can only be wrapped a couple of days beforehand at most, or they get stale. You also need to test your cookies for weather conditions. Ours had to withstand a hot and humid July, so we put a batch of already baked cookies in a one-hundred-degree oven for a few hours to make sure they would make it through the event).

They passed the test, and the display was pretty wonderful! And worth the effort.

- While lots of people have family photos, we took it to a new level. We placed green and white oversize wood-slatted frames along a forty-foot wall. The black-and-white pictures in the frames were of Liz and Dan throughout their lives. We matched their ages in double frames and had a matched picture from when they were little up to the time of their wedding. The frames were fantastic and have found their way onto the walls of several family homes to remind us of this incredible night.

- We arranged green-and-white signs in various spaces on the lawns. The sayings were charming: "Today I marry my best friend," "Family First," "Blessings," "Family Matters," and so many more.

- CLEAN golf carts were decorated with hydrangeas (they even look good in silk). Custom signs with "Just Married" announced the arrival of the bride and groom.

- The brunch that was hosted by dear friends the day after the wedding had a farmer's market theme complete with a farm stand with custom jams as take-home treats. The jars had the bride and groom's name on the labels, of course. Lizzy loves farmer's markets.

Lindsey and Craig

FEBRUARY, IN CHICAGO

In sharp contrast to Lizzy and Dan's wedding, the look and feel of Craig and Lindsey's wedding reception was over-the-top elegant. The wedding itself was incredibly beautiful and everything in the room shimmered. While it was a large event, it still had a warmth that we will always treasure.

The food was lovely and unique: passed appetizers included lobster BLTs and sweet corn and crab salad on little brioche buns. Themed specialty stations included an "Evening in Italy" with thin-crust pizza and caprese salad along with a "Sushi Bar" that featured nine different rolls. Dinner was a combination entrée of filet and lobster crab cake. Dessert included "make-your-own" ice cream sundaes, miniature homemade pies, and passed miniature desserts, including root beer floats, Dreamsicles, vanilla and red velvet "cake pops," and cheesecake lollipops dipped in dark chocolate.

The rehearsal dinner was especially personal as it was held in our home. The tables were set with our family's china and crystal. The speeches took place in our living room. The entire evening was warm and wonderful. The party at Hugo's Frog Bar the night before the wedding, and the party after the wedding reception, were pure outrageous fun. Nothing elegant, but truly a blast. The pictures tell the story.

The Rehearsal Dinner: a seated dinner party at my home
The Night Before Getting Hitched: a party at Hugo's Frog Bar
The Wedding Ceremony and Reception: the Four Seasons Hotel
The Surprise After Party: the Horseshoe Club speakeasy at the Four Seasons Hotel
The Day-After Brunch: at Craig's father's home

SPECIAL SURPRISES
FOR LINDSEY AND CRAIG

- Craig is in the business of breeding and racing thoroughbred horses, so the opening party was all about Craig and Lindsey "getting hitched." Guests were given baseball caps with our farm's logo (give people almost any kind of a hat and the party goes to a whole new level). Races our horses had won over the years were depicted on the walls of the restaurant, and Lindsey was given a gold horse pin with our colors enameled on the jockey. And the poem that we read to her was pretty darn charming. Videos of previous races (with the sound muted) played throughout the evening—amazing that we won them all! Lots of fun surprises.

- We personalized the reception rooms at the Four Seasons with pillows in the wedding colors, monogrammed with the new couple's initials. We engraved the words "Love and Luck" on mint julep cups containing chocolates, and gave the cups as the wedding favor.

- The wedding was a couple of days before February fourteenth, so we made oversize Valentine chocolates with sayings like "Be mine" and "You're the one."

- We had a custom-made wooden box carved with their names and the date—a keepsake forever. People were provided silver pens and asked to put notes (love letters) in this special box.

- An abundance of photos of Craig, Lindsey, and their families in silver frames filled the hotel's many china cabinets and at the end of the evening became fought-over keepsakes for our family.

● We set up a surprise speakeasy as the after party. We collected empty liquor bottles for months and filled them with colored water and made custom labels (on our Mac). The labels, which were all in a vintage style, included their names, their wedding date, and places and things they loved. We collected fake pearls, tommy guns, flasks, red boas, sunglasses, fedoras, and more and passed them out at random to our guests throughout the party. We bought bar stools from Indiana University and Tulane (the bride and groom's respective schools) for a corner of our speakeasy—so fun to take home for their rec room later. There was an old-time piano player, and the party was a hoot!

Farm colors in orange, black, and gold.

Barbara and Peter

APRIL, IN NASSAU, BAHAMAS

By the third wedding, we were excited to leave Chicago behind, especially during early spring when the weather is so unpredictable. This destination wedding in the Bahamas allowed our family and guests to get away to a luxurious warm-weather destination. The Ocean Club is a special paradise; the hotels and grounds are as pretty as I've ever seen.

Many Bahamian specialties were added to the menu: appetizers included cucumber cups with spiced tuna, Peking duck spring rolls, and a trio with a crab cake served on a bed of salad with watermelon and feta. Dinner entrées included roasted grouper, beef tenderloin and lobster, and giant vegetable ravioli. Desserts were a hoot: death by chocolate, coconut tapioca, chocolate shots with chocolate Pop Rocks, mango panna cotta with berry compote, Key lime pie, white chocolate shortcake, and banana Oreo cheesecake.

And the Atlantis provided us with more great venues for pre-parties and days in the sun. There were three days of sunshine and then rain on the wedding day—it happens. Just pour a little more wine and enjoy.

Small-Group First-Night Dinner: hosted by our friends at their restaurant, Luciano's

The Welcome Party on the Beach: the Cove at the Atlantis

The Rehearsal Dinner: a boating cruise

The Wedding Ceremony: on the grass at the Ocean Club

The Wedding Reception: in the formal gardens at the Ocean Club

The After Party: around the pool at the Ocean Club

LINDSEY AND CRAIG

Over-the-Top Elegance

- Black tie
- Shades of purple with silver accents
- Mirrored tabletops
- Mercury glass
- Candles everywhere
- Five differently shaped mercury-glass vases, each with distinct flowers
- Three shades of tulips, hydrangeas, hyacinths, stocks, and anemones
- Mercury-glass birds
- An indoor garden for the ceremony—greens, whites, and purples
- The garden aisle lit with candles
- Silver chairs
- Music from the first moment
- The bride chose a sweetheart-cut gown, off-the-shoulder lace
- Bridesmaids: purple sweetheart-cut gowns, bouquets in soft purples and white
- Groom and his men: black tie, traditional long silver ties
- Nine kinds of purple-wrapped candy
- Violins for the service
- Harps to greet guests
- A multiplicity of silver frames holding family photos
- Lilac gel filters over lights to cast a soft glow
- Invitations with hand-painted soft purple accents
- Trombones to lead the parade down the grand staircase
- As the bride and groom were heard to say: people always say we're overdressed—"Let's go for it!"

BARBARA AND PETER

Destination: Bahamas

- Elegant and casual
- Orchids and seashells
- Passport-themed invitation
- About one hundred people—seeking more intimacy
- Mostly young people
- Charming signage
- A magical property—multiple venues
- The Ocean Club and the Atlantis
- Four fun-filled days of celebrations
- Palm trees, ocean breezes, gardens
- The bride chose over-the-shoulder gauze and lace
- Bridesmaids: two in soft pink
- Ceremony: green orchids, cream, and a touch of pink
- Groom and his best man: dressy casual, perfect for the location
- Monkey décor integrated throughout
- White chairs, petals on the lawn
- A little glitz, a little glamour
- Added color for dinner—moving to hot color for late night
- Open-air tent in the formal gardens
- Specialty drinks at the bar
- Music, music, and more music, from classical to Bahamian
- Masses of flowers
- Dinner: Golden metallic votive candles, golden chairs
- Torches lit the way
- Bahamian touches
- Junkanoo parade—moving guests from a formal dinner to crazy fun
- Sand, boats, and lots of fun

Weddings...
A Few More Tips

...THIS IS HOW OUR STORY BEGINS

Gardens

Gardens need to look great for a wedding at home (or any party, for that matter). My daughter always hoped to get married at our home in Lake Geneva, Wisconsin. I wanted the house to look fantastic for a mid-July wedding. I walked the lakefront the previous summer and studied how certain flowers looked in mid-July and found so many of them had already started to look ragged. But I found some that were in great shape and planted appropriately for the summer of the wedding. You can't assume that what you plant will look great all summer long. Go and find examples. It's a simple trick, but so worthwhile.

Tablecloths

Simple ribbons laid across the length and width of a table in three shades of a wedding theme color can add a special look to a plain white cloth. For example, if the theme color is pink, find a pink plaid, a solid hot-pink grosgrain, and a softer pink satin all in different widths and coordinated with pink napkins—it's simply lovely.

You can also place white, gold or silver lace on top of a tablecloth. Or add a runner in any color or fabric (velvet, linen, lace, taffeta, sequin, etc.) down the middle of a long rectangular table for added color or interest.

Sometimes Buying Is as Cheap as Renting

It can almost be as cheap to buy a quilt or material as it is to rent fancy linens. We priced it and went with a custom look for Lizzy and Dan's wedding; the effect was much more to our liking.

At our Wisconsin wedding, we had the rehearsal dinner at a cute hotel overlooking Lake Geneva that had a very country-looking theme in their restaurant. In our minds, their white dinner plates just did not cut it. We bought Fiesta-style dinner plates in scarlet, sage, and sunflower for a dollar each from Walmart, and we have now used those plates thirty times since the wedding. Keep in mind that you can often buy things for less than it would cost to rent them. You will need to have someone in charge of picking up your items from the restaurant or other venue after the evening, but with access to the Internet, I would strongly encourage you to think about buying rather than renting.

Exiting the Wedding Ceremony

Toss rose petals, pom-poms, wild flowers, dried lavender, or confetti at the new Mr. and Mrs. and make sure you capture those photos. The addition of these colorful items makes a photo of the bride and groom running through their guests a real keeper. Sparklers after an evening ceremony (after dusk) are beautiful to light up the exit.

Place Cards or Not?

At a wedding, I am all for a walk-around buffet dinner with serving stations and fun things to do and see, but this style of service often makes for a shorter evening. If you want a seated meal, the question always is: do you have place cards or let people find places themselves? I am all for place cards. It allows you to control the seating of the sometimes-awkward guest, but even more importantly, it allows you to place out-of-town guests or folks who don't know many people with other people you know they will enjoy. And if you are from out of town, it is so much more comfortable to be placed at a table. The other issue is that when you allow people to seat themselves, you always need more seats than people. People take seven seats at a table for eight, and no one wants that last seat. It may be a pain in the neck, but your guests will be more comfortable if you control the seating.

Drench Those Shirts

This idea may be a little nutty, but Liz and Dan's wedding was in the height of the summer, when temperatures in Wisconsin can easily get into the nineties. The boys were wearing navy jackets with white shirts. So, you will think this is really crazy, but I wanted those boys to look crisp and clean when their jackets came off—as we all know jackets do. I went looking for white shirts, bought a few brands, and literally took a garden hose to them. Most wilted or looked "see-through," but I found a great Nordstrom brand that held up to the drenching. Those cute boys looked terrific even sopping wet in the heat. Of course, I had an extra shirt for the groom.

If You Can, Achieve a Concentration of Looks

A lot of anything can be beautiful: hundreds of balloons with strings hanging down, hundreds of votive candles or different sizes of hurricane lamps with candles, or mini lights on several dozen trees. A concentration of one element is always a wonderful look.

For most of our parties I like to concentrate color. Blue and white will always be one of my favorites, but orange and red and pinks mixed together come in a close second. Pick a color theme and let it touch everything you can from cloths, to wrappings, to signage and of course flowers. Coordination and concentration are the keys.

Favors

Food is always a great favor. Consider jams, donuts, chocolate-covered pretzels, homemade cookies in a wax bag with a custom wedding sticker; a small basket of strawberries can be charming for a rustic wedding.

Think about how you might want to wrap your favor: it can be wrapped in map paper for a destination wedding or craft paper with a colorful string for a rustic theme. Or unwrapped can be lovely with just a ribbon and a custom thank-you tag. Ribbon printed with the wedding date and the bride and groom's names looks lovely wrapped around a donut box.

Organization &
Shortcuts to Life

Get the Assumptions Agreed to First and Get Them Down on Paper

I will never forget the first ten years of my career, during which I wrote incredibly detailed marketing plans for new products. They put forth the entire war plan for whatever new brand the company was launching. These lengthy documents were critical as they established support levels that ran into the tens of millions of dollars, expectations for distribution, awareness levels at a given point in time, and a hundred other important data points, in addition to laying out what we needed to accomplish—by when and by whom. The killer was that each plan was predicated on key assumptions, and if my boss disagreed with any of the big ones, the whole plan had to be redone—and that basically entailed starting over. Really!

After a couple of years of this craziness, I pushed for a "key-assumptions document" as a new initial step for all new products. I got the "higher-ups" to agree to read the key-assumptions document and actually had my boss sign it.

This document was about three pages long, while the marketing plans could run to twenty or thirty pages. Anyway, the message here is, with just about any big project, get the assumptions agreed to first and get them in writing.

This same process has made a real difference in so many areas of my life and work. It has worked for me with building homes—getting input from all my family members early on with regard to the spaces, décor, needs—so there is no second-guessing in the middle of the building process.

I wouldn't move forward on just about anything until I had a simple outline of all that I thought everybody wanted.

With all our weddings, I wouldn't move forward on just about anything until I had a simple outline of all that I thought everybody wanted. Time was really short for us with all our weddings grouped in one year, and the assumptions were critical. Everyone has ideas. It's best to get the ideas on paper and give everyone the opportunity to give feedback and finally agree.

Legal documents, wills, and any kind of contract all have the same issue. Don't let people go off and write the entire legal document until you have a summary that lays out in simple English all you want in the final document. You will save yourself a ton of money, especially if we are talking about any sort of legal needs.

I even use this approach for family trips. This "assumptions sheet" is pretty simple: it lists when we are going; who is going; hotels, restaurants, guides, or whatever other services we will use; and even the time of dinner reservations. It's so much easier to have my grown children tell me what won't work with their little ones before I've made plans, hired transportation or other services, and invested in what I had envisioned. It may take a little while to put the assumptions in writing, but it would drive me nuts if I made all these great plans and my family didn't end up going, or had to bow out of plans that proved impractical.

It is easier to sit and talk about all of this detail face to face, and that is fine. But it will save you a whole lot of time, aggravation, and often money if you have the assumptions in writing, and everyone has agreed to them. Whether you are working with a lawyer, a contractor, an architect, a wedding planner, or doing it yourself, have someone get all those thoughts and game plans on paper, and let everyone have the chance to weigh in, make changes, and finally agree. It's a lifesaver.

EVERYTHING NEEDED

So often I receive incomplete information when I have asked for something, and it drives me a little crazy. It just creates extra work. For instance: I ask someone to investigate ordering furniture for our new offices. They come to me with a recommendation that includes the furniture and the price. Okay, great. When can we get it? The answer is, "Oh, I forgot to ask." Not good. When you are asked for just about anything, think about all the pieces and parts that may be needed, organize the information, and then present it. Coming up with a simple template on all the questions and using it for any number of things you investigate would be easy and effective.

- What is the cost?
- When will it be completed/delivered?
- Are there other options available (size, color, venues)?
- Will it meet all our needs? Are there negatives associated with this option?
- Is there a guarantee?
- When is the cancellation date?
- Do we need a deposit?
- Should photos be included?

I could go on and on. For many items, you would just write NA (not applicable), but something simple like this template helps you to get all the answers ready to go before you present something. And, by all means, know your audience. Typing up your findings is never a bad idea. If your boss is fine with just the conversation, that's also acceptable but, goodness knows, it's better to write it up anyway so you can file it away and track it later.

Photos: Delete and Edit on the Day You Take the Pic

We all love taking photos. It's so easy now on our phones to not only take pictures, but to take dozens at a time. Face it, they aren't all precious and they aren't all perfect. To keep control: **edit the photo the day you take it**. Be religious about deleting the less than great ones and take the time to edit those you want to keep. You can do it in less than thirty minutes in front of the TV or riding (as a passenger) in a car.

It's also good to have a filing system that makes your pictures easy to find. Of course, you need to send your edited pics to that file the day you take them. I can't tell you how easy it is now to look for pictures that I want when I can open my computer and see a list like this: "Cora first year" or "Alex age 1–2."

My photo inventory list now has about thirty designations...and I don't drive myself crazy with the dates they were taken. Who cares? My big list looks like this: "Craig age 1–5," "Craig age 5–10," "Craig preteen to high school," "Friends 1980–90," "Friends 1990–2000," "Wedding Lindsey and Craig," and more.

Another tip: Have hundreds—thousands—of old pictures? First, toss out half of them. Then hire a neighborhood kid one summer and have him scan all your old pics once you have sorted through and selected only the best. It is a crazy job but so worth it. Once you scan all your photos, you will still have books or boxes of pictures. Make sure you put a red dot or some mark on the back of all photos that were scanned, or you will wonder at a later date if you scanned them.

What to do with the old copies? I gave my kids a bunch of them. Then I took handfuls and put them in a big bowl on our coffee table; when friends and family come over, you should see the smiles as they sort through them. When one gets dog-eared and awful looking, it gets tossed because **all these treasures are on my computer and in the Cloud**. Once you know where they are, when you want to make a video, create a picture book for grandkids, or use them in any other way, they are all so easy to retrieve.

How Do You Eat an Elephant? One Bite at a Time

I know that in my life some of the things I have had to do simply overwhelmed me. How was I going to make this happen? I am pretty good with problems, and I can handle a great deal. But sometimes—well—I can't even describe what I was feeling. I know this sounds pretty simple but the truth is: **one bite at a time**. Once I figured this out, I could do almost anything.

Take whatever the business problem or the project is and break it up into all its many parts. I will use my real-life example: How did I manage to pull off three weddings in nine months? I did it in bite-size chunks. Take the project and lay out all the elements. For each wedding, the categories included things like: music (ceremony and dinner), transportation, flowers and other décor, favors, invitations, hotel needs, other parties, out-of-town guests, attire, menus, lighting, tents, table seating. (I could go on and on here with all the other categories, but you get the idea.) And then I would separate each of these categories into what I needed to do myself (challenge yourself: do you really need to do all that?), what could be done by others, and exactly when it needed to be completed.

I created a master list for each wedding on my computer; but I like to visually see stuff "move off my list," so I also created giant bulletin boards for each event. On my computer when the item was done or in good shape—as in no more work to be done—I turned it from black type to green. And on each wedding's bulletin board were **Post-it notes that detailed all the jobs other folks could help me do:** my daughter and my future daughters-in-law, their families, and my friends could take a job (explained on the Post-it note, which sometimes had a file to go with it), complete it, and report back. I know it sounds a bit nuts, but moving those notes from the top side of the board to the bottom, where all things completed were placed, was important. While our boards showed all that was left to do, it was also really motivating to see what we had accomplished.

When you are overwhelmed with a project: 1) **figure out who can help you and don't be afraid to ask,** 2) **if need be, hire competent help**, and 3) create the master list and **break the project into bite-size chunks**. Just taking the time to do this lowers your blood pressure. I have used this process when creating a new brand, building a home, starting a charity from scratch, and merging two organizations. With almost any big endeavor, it helps.

For Any Project, Memorialize the Experience

We all think we will remember details about vendors and service providers who do work for us, but frankly I don't. If you do, your memory is way better than mine.

So when I use a vendor or tradesperson, I have a "great/good" list and a "do not use again" list. A couple of years after the fact, I will often remember the names from a specific project, but I am not positive if that was the electrician I loved or the one who caused us all the trouble.

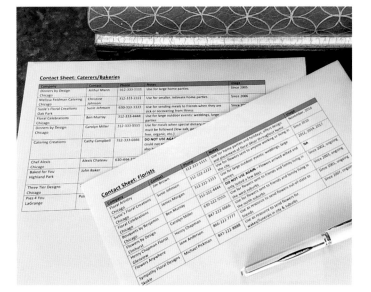

Visit gatherasyougo.com to view a sample contact sheet.

It is easy if you **keep a list of vendors you use, with ratings.** I use a simple contact sheet:

- Name of vendor
- Who recommended them to me
- What they did
- The quality of the job

It may sound obsessive-compulsive, but I do it for everyone who performs a service: tradespeople, caterers, music groups, florists—you get the idea. Once again, it just makes life easier.

Keep a Copy

Never give your boss (or anyone) the only copy of anything. Never keep something important on only one computer. Always keep a hard copy or a copy in the Cloud. It's just smart.

Always keep a hard copy or a copy in the Cloud.

Do the Homework before You Begin the Creative Process

After decades of working with graphic designers, florists, architects, and all kinds of creative folks, I know that it is easier to get the end product I'm seeking if I give these creative people clear direction up front. I always do a "white paper" if it is for a big project like building a home, holding a wedding, or designing a logo that needs to last a new brand for its lifetime. But equally as important, I work hard to SHOW these creative people what I think looks great.

If I am building a home, I have a binder with sections for each room. I have photos of interiors and exteriors. I have photos of ceilings I prefer as well as the type of doors and light fixtures (there's a whole lot more on the building of a home in the Decorating chapter). When the project is a wedding, I show the florist designs I think are lovely, and I also show them things I don't like at all. It's just as critical to show the creative folks the "don't likes" as the designs you love.

Be careful about the photos of things that you like. Put things in order of priority so you don't overwhelm people. When you're working on new packaging, this is equally important. Show the graphic artists the feel of the packages you want. Show them examples of where the logo is prominent and appealing. As they say, a picture is worth a thousand words but, even more importantly, you have taken the time to help the creative process along the way. Your end result will be easier to attain. You'll save money, because all too often, people have to go through multiple iterations before they are happy. **Do the work up front to SHOW them what you love**, and you are far more likely to love the end result.

Examples of what you might show if you want an "orange wedding."

WHAT TO TAKE
AND WHO WANTS WHAT

·························

Whether you're cleaning out Grandma's house or going through your own home, photograph every furniture item in each room. I know this sounds like a lot of work but, trust me, over the life of this big project it is worth it. Once you photograph everything—chairs, rugs, tables, artwork, every major thing—print the pictures. I made duplicate binders containing the photos and the measurements of almost all the items for each of my kids when we were moving from our home of thirty years. Anything I was willing to give away went into their binders. I divided the binder by sections: 1) chairs, 2) tables, 3) couches, 4) artwork, etc. Each of my kids was asked to put their initials on anything they might want. When their books came back to me, a whole bunch of stuff had only one set of initials; for the rest, we sat together and they compromised. **This approach was so much easier, especially when people don't have the time to get together or are in different parts of the world.** It's also so easy to divide up what is left over and to make a donations pile. This enabled us to e-mail the pics to friends who I knew had kids setting up new apartments. (While everything is still in your house, these pictures are also an important record for your homeowner's insurance in the event of damage or loss.)

Each of my kids was asked to put their initials on anything they might want.

And of course, if all your kids are in the same town, it is easy to have them each put a different color of painter's tape (which won't ruin surfaces, while stickers are hard to get off) on anything they may want, and you can box it up or ship it. But it is still a great idea to have photos and measurements of all the stuff you will put into storage.

These photographs also come in handy when you are moving to a new home and want to use a lot of your existing furniture. Add the measurements of each piece to the photo. When placing the old favorites on the new furniture plan, you can sort through your chairs, sofas, and tables and find the ones you like and the ones that, more importantly, FIT.

Just Good Advice

Interesting Conversations and Making a Connection

Some people are so good at "chitchat"; I am not. I prefer real conversations with meaning, controversy, humor, passion, or something you can take with you. I love it when you can really get people talking. I took a bunch of teenagers on vacation once with another mom. We had dinners every night, and each day they were on their own. At dinner, we posed different questions. It was fascinating to hear their answers; they shared experiences and insights, and it was really fun to listen. I can't imagine having had five nights of chitchat. Over those five dinners, we got to know those kids so much better and built connections with them that have lasted for decades.

I love "connecting" with people I care about on trips or at an occasion as simple as a dinner party. If the guests don't know each other, I always ask each to tell a little about themselves—and then I softly encourage a time limit.

I often use the "questions game" at dinner parties. I mix people up, meaning I sit people together who don't know each other well. My friends come from many different places and from different lines of work, religions, and income brackets. They've experienced different traumas and tragedies and have different passions. They bring all this to the table when they engage in conversation.

Taking conversations beyond the surface level isn't always easy. People feel comfortable at the surface, and moving deeper often entails a bit of risk. But the most rewarding relationships and conversations tend to happen when you move beyond the surface. You might just make a great new friend.

Almost any question works as a starter, but here is a short sample:

- Who do you love most in the world and why?
- If you could have any job anywhere, what would it be?
- What is the most embarrassing thing that ever happened to you?
- You get one "do-over." What is it?
- Which of your parents influenced you the most and why?
- You are given three million dollars, and you have to give it away. What will you do?
- You can fix one major thing in this world. What will it be?
- You have a month's sabbatical during which you will go and help a charity. What will it be and why?
- If there were one thing about you that you could change, what would it be?

I often use the "questions game" at dinner parties.

To Make It Memorable, Make It Personal

Whether it's your team at work, your family, or your best friends, know what they favor. In fact, know what all their favorites are. Make a list: their favorite meal, dessert, candy, snack, music, author, activities, what their "best day ever" might be, their initials, their sizes, etc. Discover their favorite color, sports team, flower, their kids' names or grandkids' names, and anything else you want to gather. It will come in very handy.

Imagine you have totally stressed out your team at work. Surprise them with their favorite treats. Chocolate chip cookies for some, hot popcorn for others—whatever their favorites are. After a particularly tough day, I had personalized treats brought in to a late meeting. It got us recharged and refocused, and the personalization was truly appreciated. This simple effort said I cared.

I once had a surprise birthday celebration for a wonderful friend. The meal was all of her favorite food brought in from four different restaurants. The table was set with her colors. The photos that decorated the room were of her kids and grandkids. The flowers were her favorite. And her gift was a weekend at her favorite hotel. It was a special day.

And how do you discover people's favorites and gather all this information? Simply ask (for employees, I actually make asking these questions part of the HR process) and create a list for future reference.

Whether it's your team at work, your family, or your best friends, know what they favor.

It's All About the Time

No one has enough time. But it is critical that for some things, such as creating connections, you make the time. Here are three examples from my life.

YPO (THE YOUNG PRESIDENTS' ORGANIZATION)

One of my all-time best moves was to join YPO. I have belonged to the same YPO forum group for decades. These folks are invaluable and eight of the best people in my world. **Getting counsel from like-minded professionals you trust is one of the best gifts you can give yourself.** When you are lucky enough to find this kind of situation, these folks will challenge you and help you grow: their push-back is simply fantastic.

CHARITY BOARDS

You may have a career and kids. You really don't think you have time for community service. I would urge you to make the time. The associations I have made while serving the community have been incredibly powerful in my life and my career. Fellow board members from the three not-for-profits for which I work are my biggest supporters and, equally importantly, I get to see how they think. I see their values in action.

I call on these people most often for help. They are independent. They don't count on me to grow their careers, and they don't have political motivation. They are just incredibly smart people who have become mentors. If you are on a not-for-profit board and don't respect and admire the people with whom you work, try another one. **You want to do more than just help; you want to be in a place where you can grow too.**

FRIENDSHIPS

Keep your friends. Most of us don't have time anymore for the "every Thursday night out," with the girls (or guys), but I would urge you to do something incredibly wonderful for yourself once a year, like taking a trip with your friends. You need them. Life can get mighty hard, and in life's tough times your friends will be your personal board.

When you are asking for help, use the right language. Be specific: "Hi, Tom. I was hoping you could help me think out loud about something. I only need an hour of your time."

Don't burn bridges. It's a very small world. People you used to work with can be amazing mirrors.

Build solid connections. If you don't have people in your life with whom you can talk, work hard to create those relationships and to keep them.

SURFACE RELATIONSHIPS
ARE NOT FOR ME

I don't know if there is a lesson here, but it's a real part of who I am. I don't do well with what I call "surface" relationships. I have many wonderful friends, most of whom will share their joys and their sorrows, and we will work through them together. How can you trust someone with your "stuff" when they don't share theirs? Over the years we have built tremendous trust.

I don't do well at cocktail parties. And I don't love sitting next to folks I don't know at a dinner party when it is all small talk. I love to really get to know people. That is probably why I play the "questions game" I wrote about earlier in this chapter in the story titled "Interesting Conversations and Making a Connection."

I have found myself, for weekends at a time, with people who live only at a surface level. They talk about golf, tennis, or restaurants—and by the end of the weekend, I want to run away fast and stay away. Life is too short for me to talk only about where we eat and what our golf scores may be. We all have "stuff," some of us more than others, **but the ability to connect with people is a gift and one that I cherish**. I believe the only way to really build a deep connection with people is to share and to be willing to receive what others have to share, and there is nothing in this world more important to me than the deep and very real relationships I have with my family and friends.

So, About those Relationships at Work:

Years ago I read about "intimate distance." This concept recognizes that knowing the folks with whom you work—understanding who they are and what is important to them—will strengthen the relationships at work significantly and lead to a better working environment. But the concept draws the line at becoming "every weekend" friends—getting together regularly, playing tennis, or traveling together. Observing that distance protects the work relationship. For the most part I have followed this—but I will say that some of the people with whom I have worked have become lifelong friends on whom I count and cherish.

LAUGH—AND BUILD
A CLOSER CONNECTION

My son Craig and his wife, Lindsey, were visiting in Lake Geneva. They have this lovable, crazy golden labradoodle we call Ni Ni (her real name is Lanai after the island in Hawaii where they honeymooned). We have had dogs all our lives, and I LOVE dogs, but at my house, our sweet pups do not sleep on the sofas or on our beds. At Lindsey and Craig's house, they are welcome to land anywhere they please. So, at a shared family home where there are lots of new babies—and when another of my kids is not used to dogs sleeping on the same sofa where we take naps or we lay down a new infant—we shoo Ni Ni to move to the great new dog bed we bought and placed near us on the floor.

So, a few minutes after the "shooing of Ni Ni," this loveable dog comes trotting out of the side of the house where my bedroom is and she smells "a little off." Lindsey and I both jump up and run to my bedroom, where Ni Ni has had a giant bout of diarrhea all over my yellow and white rug. My cute daughter-in-law is about to lose it as she is also pregnant (and more than emotional at the time). She insists she will clean it up. Needless to say, we bonded even more with our pots of hot water and soap as we scrubbed out Ni Ni's latest gift from my rug. We were rolling with laughter and NO, it wasn't all that funny, but in fact it was: the two of us were laughing at the absurdity of this crazy dog and trying to combine our lives in a way that would make both of us happy. I love this girl more every day. **The more times we bond over the next mess or problem, the more we build a connection.** Put away your irritation. Keep in mind that what counts in life is the connection to people you love.

I will tell you that Ni Ni had me change my decorating thoughts for the new house. Everything in it would be able to withstand the abuse of three dogs, loads of little kids, and any other kind of mess we would throw at it. It's easier to plan fabrics, rugs, and couches when you know right up front you don't have much of a chance for "light and pretty" to survive the havoc of happy families and all that comes with them. I will say I love our new home now that it's finished, and you can't find the dirt anywhere. But I promise you it is there—it's just well hidden.

ON BECOMING
A HERO

I'm having lunch with one of my executives, a great guy with wonderful personal values who ran our HR department at Alberto.

He tells me his wife is driving him crazy: she wants to build a new home close to where they're living, and then he'll have to go through the "agony" of moving. He tells me he's planning to cause her grief for the next year before he eventually gives in.

Now I know that Doug adores his wife, and they have a fantastic marriage. So I look at him and say, "Doug??? Let's go next-door to Amling's [a flower and landscaping shop] and pick up a lovely new flowering bush. Then why don't you write a lovely note to your sweet wife and take home the note, the bush, and a bottle of champagne and celebrate your new house decision. Instead of being a pain for the next year, you can be an absolute hero, and she'll talk about this for the rest of her life."

After a few minutes of convincing he decided to do just that. It's a story they tell over and over. Let me ask you, **what's the gain in causing someone you love a year of pain?**

Instead of being a pain for the next year, you can be an absolute hero.

Here's to our new home

With thoughts from

Scott Mordell
Chief Executive Officer, YPO*

Many people can say they are a better person today because they know Carol. I am one of them.

We have been meeting every month for more than twenty years in a YPO forum, a small group of CEOs committed to personal growth, honesty, open sharing of ideas, and accepting each other without judgment. Our meetings are important for us to actively reflect on our experiences, thoughts, actions, and futures. For me, our journey together has been a spiritual journey as much as one of business and personal learning. The regular reflection in a safe setting has helped this group become like a church experience for me.

Life can be described as ten percent what happens to us and ninety percent how we react. We all control our own behavior, and our ultimate happiness is determined from within. We are at our best when our actions align with who we are at our core. With the noise of life, we need others to help us find and apply our best selves.

A life well lived proves to be relevant and make a positive difference in the lives of other people. Sharing our wisdom gained through experience is invaluable. "At My Core" is the foundation Carol has lived, demonstrated, and helped me learn. May we all carry the tradition forward.

* YPO is a peer-learning community of more than 25,000 CEOs across 130 countries, committed to becoming better leaders and better people. It was formerly known as Young Presidents' Organization.

Lessons from My Mom

We all go through life living by certain rules, and probably, as importantly, by having a "built-in" understanding of the right way to do things. The "right way" isn't written down, and no one has sat you down and had "the conversation" laying out all the rules at one time: you just have an understanding of the lessons you grew up with. As I've been putting this book together, I've been reflecting on some of those lessons, and I realize they came to me primarily from my mom—and through her, from my grandma. They were both working women at a time when not all that many women worked outside the home. And from them I have learned a lot:

- Feelings matter.
- Character is doing what's right when no one is looking.
- The good things in life are meant to be shared.
- A positive attitude is a powerful tool.
- Kindness is key.
- We must leave things better for people who will follow us.
- Credibility is absolutely everything. If you tell the truth, you don't have to remember anything.
- I can't change other people no matter how right I am or how hard I try; I can only change myself.
- No matter how tough it gets, stand tall and handle it with dignity and grace.
- Showing vulnerability will bring people closer, and people are more likely to trust you.
- You can be feminine, fun, silly, and a best friend at the same time the world recognizes all your success.
- Be grateful for all you have—never guilty.
- Love your family above all else.

Lessons from My Dad

My dad was an entrepreneur at heart. He was one of those people who not only had a vision, but was exceptional at making it happen. There are so many words that come to mind when I think of him: resourceful, feisty, fun-loving, passionate about making a difference, and hard-headed. And I was in awe of how much he adored my mom; they had an incredible love affair for sixty years.

My dad focused on taking risks that enriched our lives and made our business and careers much more rewarding. He had many "sayings"; the ones I'm sharing here have stayed with me, and I've embraced them all. To this day, my dad, at age ninety-seven, still inspires me with great thoughts and kind words; he has a ton of love to give and spoils us all with his generosity.

- Think BIG. It takes just as much time to develop a big idea as a small idea.
- Always keep your foot on first base.
- Your health, your family, and a job you enjoy: THAT is what life is all about.
- You can't grow by sitting in an office. Get out there and help.
- Open your home, open your heart. Share and be kind.
- The harder you work the luckier you get.
- Family takes care of family—even when it drives you nuts.
- You have to speculate to accumulate. (A statement credited to P. G. Wodehouse.)
- You can do anything you put your mind to (girls can too!).
- Read, Read, Read.
- Playing with your grandkids (and great-grandkids) is way more fun than giving them M&M's.
- Take time out to play.
- Making money is nice but it's not why you work: you work to build something you can be proud of.
- There is no place better EVER than America.
- Sometimes you just have to fight. You might be small (our company) but don't let the big guys push you around.
- The lawyers are not always right. Get their opinions, but business people should run the business.
- A positive attitude is a powerful tool and winners will make it happen (losers *let* it happen).

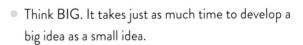

Keys to Becoming Successful: Passion and Priorities

These words are taken from various speeches I have given over the years to young people. Perhaps this advice will be helpful to you or someone you love.

I hope to convince you that whatever you choose to do, wherever you end up—if you are a teacher, an accountant, start a business out of your garage, or end up as a major corporate executive—it is your passion and dedication that can take you to great places. To be ready for the good or the very difficult, there are two words that summarize what you need to succeed: **Passion and Priorities**. And this is true whether you are well launched on a career or just starting out.

Let me begin with priorities. I believe that everyone should have a personal mission statement and that this simple statement can be a vital key to your success. Corporations have mission statements that articulate what they stand for and what they hope to accomplish. Each of you needs that kind of focus: a personal mission that lets you judge each decision, each action, each goal and next step. It needn't be elaborate, it doesn't have to follow a format, and it won't be published; it's a guide that will make your decisions easier and your goals more clear.

Get gut-wrenchingly honest with yourself. A mission is a sense of where you want to focus, where you want to go, not what you're willing to give up. What do you really want to dedicate yourself to? What is first: family, church, fun, money, power, recognition, giving back, the ability to be creative? Is geography key? Must you maximize your income immediately? What series of skills do you want to hone? How can you become indispensable to your company and still have fun and feel rewarded? Those are the core issues of a personal mission statement. You may not know now exactly what you want to do with your life, but you do have values and thoughts. Let them guide you.

Remember, what we're talking about is a roadmap, not a straitjacket. The unexpected will happen, both the victories and the disappointments. There may be life-changing experiences that cause you to draw up a new mission. This statement is simply a way for you to prioritize and address issues in your life, not to exclude and ignore.

Once you've decided on your mission, pursue it with passion and commitment. A mission without passion is a crutch. It's a rationalization, not a roadmap. Look about you. See the opportunities. Stand out and be heard. And remember the role of a mission and the importance of passion in everything you attempt.

- If you want to develop new products, marshal the resources, prepare for doubters, and ramrod the products to market.
- If you believe as I do that the unchecked distribution of guns is putting our society at risk, find groups working for change and share your passion.
- If you believe that we can be providing better health care to a broader spectrum of people, support with passion those working in that direction.
- If your focus is family, you don't need to proclaim it, you need to show it. You need to set the moral and ethical standards that establish the foundation. If you want honesty in the family, you need to treat every issue, regardless of how uncomfortable, with openness and truth.

Keys to Success in Business (and Life)

One of the questions most often asked is, "What does it take to succeed in business?" It's also a question often asked by new employees: "What does it take to succeed in this company?" After hearing some variation of these questions several dozen times, I put together a list that I use in speeches, in interviewing candidates, or at new employee orientations.

- **Attitude is key.** The person who is committed passionately to the success of our business—who has an I-Can-Do-It attitude—will succeed. One person can make a tremendous difference, and it's up to you to demonstrate that you are one of those people.

- **Fight for your ideas and do something big.** The best idea can disappear without a strong advocate. Take the lead in making a difference.

- **Nice guys don't finish last; they win!** Aggressive and passionate shouldn't equate with unpleasant—ever. The higher you rise, the more pleasant and understanding you need to be. Never underestimate the value of thanks and the value of recognition. Ego has no place in business. If you have one, lose it.

- **My job is to do whatever it is that needs to be done.** If someone needs you to cover so they can participate in a team-building exercise, do it. If it's collating sales material, help out. Be proactive. Lend a hand. People notice.

- **Credibility is everything**. Some of the most important, career-saving words I have ever heard are, "I don't know." **Never, ever fake it.** If you're wrong, admit it and correct it. If you've made a mistake, fix it and learn from it. If it's going to take some time to find an answer, set a timetable and stick to it.

- **If you never fail, you'll never grow.** If it's always comfortable and easy, you can't know the big win. You will learn best when you are being stretched.

Don't sit back. Reach out, get involved, and take a risk. When I interview a candidate I always ask, "Is there anything you wish you hadn't done? Is there anywhere you failed at something you tried?" The best talent has a ton to tell me. Those individuals who have softball answers either never took the risk or don't meet one of my key values—that of honesty.

- **When you're furious with others, look inside and see if you're really dissatisfied with yourself.** A person who always lays blame is soon cut out of team activities.

- **Love what you're doing**. If you don't, you probably won't be successful. And even if you are successful, you'll be miserable—so what's the point?

- **Complaining gets you nowhere** and people (especially in business) simply don't want to hear it. So, it's best to just keep quiet and figure out how you can fix whatever it is, and if you can't change it, try changing how you think about it.

- **Match your values and aspirations**. You're not just looking for a place to work; you are looking for a home.

- **Have the courage to do what is right**, even when it's not popular, and to chase your dreams with passion and unwavering tenacity.

- **Give back**. Our communities are not perfect. They are the responsibility of business, government, and each of us. If you don't commit to making a difference, who will?

PHILOSOPHY ON LIFE:

90 PERCENT IS AN A

Just as it's impossible for friends and family to be GREAT all the time, the same goes for employees.

Here's an example from our business:

My mother called me into her office one day and was really upset about a raise our vice president of human resources was giving to an employee. I was president of our consumer products business at the time, and we had more than 3,500 employees in the unit. My mother had run HR in the old days, and she still kept an eagle eye on our systems and frequently brought "stuff" to my attention (and drove me a little nuts—FAMILY BUSINESS!). She asked me if I thought the raise was right, and frankly, I looked over the data and said, "No. I think it is too high." She smiled and told me to call in our vice president to change it. And I told her I wouldn't do that. I would stick with the VP's decision. I didn't want to review 3,500 individuals— and as long as the VP and I agreed the vast majority of the time, it was okay and I would let it stand. **Ninety percent is an A.** Believe me, it is a whole lot less stressful to live your life without expecting perfection from everyone. Forgiveness is a pretty good tool too.

Family Meetings

....

We have regularly scheduled family meetings, and they have become very important to all of us. I began this process a little more than a decade ago when my youngest child was about twenty and my oldest was in his late twenties. I probably should have started them earlier, but the timing corresponded with the breakup of my marriage, so I didn't have to "consult" anyone about having these meetings or what I wanted to share and how I wanted to nurture my family going into the future.

I could write a long chapter about what we do and why, but here are a few of the important things I want to pass along.

These meetings are a time when we come together to share and openly talk about big issues. My kids are all in different kinds of businesses. It was important to me to talk openly and agree to common business practices no matter what their chosen field. We have built a family reputation, and I wanted to talk about what that means to all of us, even when some business practices might allow you to take advantage of certain opportunities. For instance, when we create a new business, we will form a limited liability company (LLC) so we can protect most of our assets from any liability arising from this new business. If one of our LLCs were to go into bankruptcy, we may have the legal right to walk away from our obligations to any unsecured creditors—but we as a family are not going to do that. Our relationships with our banking partners and other creditors are way more important to us over the long term, as is our family reputation. I needed to make sure my kids understood that.

When we first started our family meetings, I wrote a letter to my children. I reminded them of our family history, where my parents came from, and their backgrounds. I reminded them that neither my family nor their dad's family, when they started out, had anywhere near the assets and advantages that our family now enjoys. The letter spoke of the importance of reputation, hard work, kindness, tenacity, and much more. It continues to serve as an important foundation to the way we live our lives.

At the time, we did not have a document that stated our family values. So we wrote one, and we included not only our values, but also examples of our values in action. My three children and I have lived our values over the decades of growing our family. But over the last five years, we have added three wonderful new "in-law kids" to our family. I am incredibly fortunate as I truly love them all. My children have wonderful partners, and there are now six grandchildren, with each family having two kids. So, we took the time a couple of years ago to review and restate our family values. What a wonderful thing to have all these young people with their new families on the same page as me. I am so proud of the work we did. In the process, we examined our hopes and dreams of what our family will look like in the years ahead. We spoke about what we want from our relationships with each other, our goals for their children, how we will impact the community, personal business goals, and more. I know that goals cause one to focus, and revisiting these and updating them over the years will be a very good thing. The reinvigorated family values document is vital to our future.

As I have said, we have significant means with which to do whatever we wish, and we will be able to pass significant funds on to our kids and hopefully to their children as well. My parents and I worked incredibly hard to build our assets. I have worked for forty years (and continue to do so), and my parents worked for two decades longer than that. But we fully acknowledge we are also incredibly lucky, and we are thankful. We take great pride in all our philanthropic efforts. As my children share this passion, we talk about our philanthropy; we wrote a third document that states our thoughts and goals regarding philanthropy, and it supports our continuing efforts—to positively impact our communities.

One last point that I think is important, although I suspect some people may not agree. My kids know their financial pictures now and into the future. Of course, I have the right to change my mind, and they are fully aware of that, but the overall game plan is shared at our family meetings, and we talk about its implications. They know the major gifts that I will make, and there are no big secrets. They don't have access to all these funds, as much of it is in trust or controlled by me. But I fully believe this knowledge helps them to build their lives and futures, and helps to eliminate all the "what ifs." Knowing the long-term plan allows them to be able to make fully informed choices as they plan their futures. My children look forward to these meetings and participate fully.

*My advice:
talk to your kids
about all things meaningful.
It builds better relationships
and honesty among the family.*

The Fun of Giving It Away NOW

I think I told you: I am a "things" person. In my will, a lot of stuff has been designated for people. I love my friends; some of them are as close to me as family. So instead of waiting to give away everything when I die, I am having fun giving some of it away now. It is such an incredible kick to share things with people when I can see their faces.

I've put a new car in a friend's garage, anonymously arranged for a scholarship for a child's education, and been silently "there" when a neighbor has run into trouble (I've used their clergy to pass along monetary help). And when I see someone I care about in need (and they were already in my will), I figure NOW is the time to help. It's a good thing for both of us.

I have given monetary gifts to some dear friends— large enough to make a statement, but not so large that I can't still give them more while I walk this earth. What a hoot that is. I called my best girlfriends together, and we had dinner. Several had to come in from out of state. I told them I needed them and that it was important. Then I wrote them a letter—the same letter for each. It basically said that I had a gift to give each of them, but if anyone didn't accept the gift, the others would not get it either. I had known that some of these friends would have a hard time accepting my generosity, but they could really use the help. This way I knew they would "have to" accept the gift, or they would be depriving others. These gifts were lifesavers for a few of my friends at the time. How lucky for me that I could help them while I was still alive. Okay, so you might not have the resources I do. But you sure can make a difference in people's lives now, and you sure can share something of yourself. Think about a book you love, furniture in your home, a set of dishes or candlesticks. Or think about putting up the money to get them a cleaning service once a month. Why wait?

Being Grounded has Nothing to Do with Money

When my children were very young, an acquaintance came into our home and, while standing at my front door, looked around and said something like, "How can your kids be so grounded with all of this?" I was hurt at first, but I put it aside. It is twenty-plus years later, but I will always remember that comment. This man and his family are now among my all-time closest friends. His daughter became my daughter's best buddy, and his wife is like a sister to me. We all had some serious growing to do.

My mom said this to me when I was still in school: **"Love people for who they are, not what they have."** This has been a key value in our lives forever and one that I have worked hard to successfully pass on to my children. Being grateful for all we have and sharing it makes life work for me and makes it all so much more special.

And always stay humble and kind (a great Tim McGraw song). Our friends come from all walks of life: some are billionaires, and some have modest resources. We love them all equally and learn from everyone. There is nothing I hate more than a fat ego or a showy personality.

The Whole Truth and Nothing but the Truth

Alberto Culver had decided to separate our two businesses, the Sally Beauty Company and our consumer products business. Their business models were in conflict in that Sally's biggest customers were Alberto's biggest competitors, and Alberto's biggest customers were retailers that were competitors with our Sally Beauty stores. We had made  a deal to sell Sally to the Regis Corporation (a large operator of beauty salons under names like Supercuts and Regis, and a manufacturer of products sold in their salons). Our deal was announced, but a couple of months before the deal was to close, Alberto pulled out. We had a major breakup fee to pay, but my board and I were positive it was the right thing to do.

We were in a tough predicament. We needed to find another partner, and we needed to do it fast. Merrill Lynch brought the private equity investment firm of Clayton, Dubilier and Rice (CDR) to our attention. They were interested in talking. Goldman Sachs had been our banker on the previous failed deal, so they too were involved. We all met in New York at the offices of CDR. The meeting was going very well, and the next step would have been to have CDR go to Sally to do more due diligence. Before I would let that happen I had something very important to share. I told the CDR folks there was a strong possibility that one of our biggest suppliers at Sally was going to pull their products from our Sally stores. It was also likely they would drop us as a major distributor to salons. Losing this supplier would have a huge impact, and given the fact that it was not yet a fait accompli, some parties to the discussions were very upset that I shared the information with CDR.

As executive chairman of Alberto Culver, there was no way I was letting more disruption happen at Sally, and no way I would let CDR into our offices to meet with our people if they were not aware of this possibility and willing to go forward despite this risk. The CEO of CDR asked me to join him in his office, and we talked privately. It was a huge issue—and one that had caught them by surprise. We left New York with CDR's promise that we would hear from them later; they had some thinking to do. As it turned out we did move forward. We completed a Reverse Morris Trust deal with CDR. Sally Beauty would become a stand-alone public company, as would our consumer products business under the name Alberto Culver.

CDR thought they could keep the major supplier we had spoken of. It wasn't to be the case. This company pulled their business a couple of months after our deal had closed. The lesson, of course, is always **do the right thing**. Full transparency was the only way to handle this critical situation. Can you imagine the repercussions if CDR had not known of this issue? Can you imagine the lawsuits that would have ensued? As the years went by, the Sally business actually got stronger. And despite the loss of this major piece of business, Sally thrived, as did its stock price.

Sometimes There Is No Compromise

I heard an awful story on the radio one morning about a mentally challenged child being beaten by his foster parents because he wouldn't stop asking for another hot dog. This story came to the news station via a neighbor whose own child monitor system had picked up and recorded this situation from an apartment in the same building. The police were called, and this awful story made all the news stations in Chicago. I found out later that morning that the accused parents worked for us at Alberto. I was shell-shocked. Not only did they work for us, but they were longtime employees who worked in our factory and had been on several of our important committees. That morning they were both in jail, but they would be out on bail shortly. My head of HR told me I had to allow them to return to work. They were innocent until proven guilty. There was no way I was letting those people back into our building. We prided ourselves on family values and helping people less fortunate than ourselves. That tape recording was clear, and that horrific situation had been broadcast all over the news.

I insisted the employees be put on paid leave. I was told that our union would put forth a grievance and that, if the tape recording from the child monitoring system was not admitted as evidence in the trial, the couple might get off, and we would owe them all sorts of money for our refusal to allow them to return to work. Well, this went on for many months, and I held my ground. I was visited by our HR department many times telling me what the financial implications could be if these folks were not convicted. Sometimes there is no compromise. It turned out the tape recording was admitted in the trial, and both our employees were convicted and were going to spend some serious time in jail. I guess in some ways that was lucky for me because of the stand I had taken. But, frankly, nothing else made sense to me and when you talk about the culture of a company I believe it is really important to say what you mean and stand by what you say.

Once again, do the right thing.

"When you talk about the culture of a company I believe it is really important to say what you mean and stand by what you say."

CHAPTER 07

Capturing Memories & Gifting

Of course, the greatest gift in life is friendship, but how wonderful it is to be able to remind your friends and loved ones that you care and are thinking of them by sending or bringing along a little gift. Gifts can range from photographs, to poetry, to giving a charitable donation in someone's name, to gifts of service. Creating something homemade or having something custom made in someone's honor is incredibly special. I love to surprise people with a gift for a special occasion or make a small dinner party more fun by wrapping party favors. My mom loved to give gifts, and she passed on the tradition. I know I get more pleasure from giving a gift than from receiving one. One of my favorite sayings will always be "The gift is to the giver."

Very Clever Gifting

Each of the people we love, each of the people we touch, has special moments in their lives. They can be momentous, life-changing moments like a birth or an adoption. They can be career-changing events like a big promotion or a new job. They can also be milestones like the first day of school or, of course, birthdays or anniversaries.

To reach out to your friends to recognize and share those moments adds, for them and for you, another touch of something special. A frame for the first picture of a new baby, a toy or book that had meaning to your kids, or something your mother gave to you can have tremendous meaning to a new parent. School supplies for a budget-strained teacher or student in need can jumpstart a school year. Pajamas, a bathrobe, slippers or a blanket can show a recuperating patient that you are sharing their journey. And, of course, there are dozens of ways to enhance the meaning of birthdays and anniversaries.

Never overlook the gift of time. For the new mother, babysitting time for the infant or for other siblings...or for the recuperating patient, meals or housekeeping may be a greatly appreciated gift—and a touch of relief.

A treat someone would never buy for themselves is always exciting. And occasionally for no reason other than "thinking of you," a personal or silly gift can bring a very special moment of joy for the recipient and for you.

I have found that homemade gifts of the heart are often the best.

Here are a few ideas—feel free to borrow any and all!

Pay for ten basketballs at a local Boys and Girls Club.

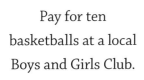

Fund a free lunch for one hundred kids—easy to do at just about any charitable organization.

Plant a garden, tulip bulbs, or a tree in someone's honor; almost any school will accommodate you.

Send an underprivileged kid to camp.

Adopt a dog or cat in someone's name at a local animal shelter.

Make a quilt out of your child's baby clothes—or make two, so that you and your child can each have one.

Have family photos transferred to a blanket—so special for an older person.

Etch a wedding invitation or a family tree on a crystal vase or block.

Check out custom "chalkboards" on the Internet. They're so easy and so clever! Create one for your young kids or grandkids and then frame it.

Fill half a tackle box with mini cars for the little boy in your life who loves vehicles. Use flat-topped cars so the box closes. This gift was a total hit with my grandson. Don't fill the tackle box completely, as it is super fun to give "one more little car" when the child comes to visit or for a special occasion.

Treasure your mom's keepsakes. My mom had a beautiful bracelet and when she passed away it came to me. I had the bracelet taken apart and made sets of earrings for my closest friends and family. I never would have worn the bracelet but these earrings are precious to everyone. While we are talking about my mom, I picked out about twenty-five gifts—purses, scarves, jewelry—and sent them to friends of hers and mine. They were so appreciated by all.

Make a calendar of old photos.

Give a pretty decorated box filled with cards for all occasions. Everyone needs cards; my friends have really loved this one.

Send a fully planted outdoor pot for a patio: it's an amazing gift when it just shows up at someone's front door.

Buy holiday-themed dish towels or fingertip towels that look like they go together (as in the same color, the same size, or a coordinated design). It's also fun to do the same with bibs for a new baby. When someone you know is pregnant, start collecting bibs for the various holidays.

Find fantastic containers and give them to your florist to use when you send flowers. Choosing the containers makes the presentation a little more special.

Write a check to a charity with the amount filled in but leave the designation line blank; let friends decide where to use it.

Give college students gift cards for their favorite college-town restaurants. Punch a hole in a corner of each card and connect them all with a simple key ring or ribbon. Date night, late night, after the big game—those gift cards will come in handy!

Do something outrageous: kidnap a friend for a trip, hire a cleaning service for four sessions and give it to someone who is feeling overwhelmed, go in with your family and buy the massage chair for your dad (just go ahead and deliver it; I promise it will be used).

Just show up with dinner.

Share a list of your favorite books with your favorite readers…send it with popcorn.

Buy a fun beach tote and embroider a great saying on it.

Découpage a large wooden "treasure chest" by gluing and sealing stickers, cutouts, photos, and other mementos with Mod Podge. Fill the chest with little prizes. (My daughter is a first-grade teacher; I did this for her, and she LOVED it.)

Buy a cozy throw and embroider it with anything from initials to a favorite saying.

Give a set of poker chips in an engraved case— a great gift for a man.

Give a gift that embraces a lifetime: a wooden plaque in the shape of an American flag, with the recipient's many achievements written in as part of the flag's design. (For beautiful gifts like this, check out Sticks at sticks.com. They're costly, but a lifetime-achievement gift is great for a retirement.)

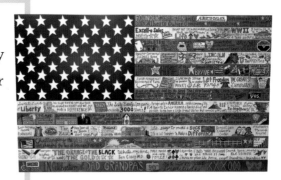

Create a book of memories. One of the most treasured gifts given to my family was a bound book that, in several hundred pages, featured the most important aspects of our lives, including our family roots, the building of a company, the births of our children, the building of a racing stable, and the charities we honor.

Place outrageous feather boas in a box for your glamorous friend on her fortieth birthday.

Write a poem for a special occasion. Present it on beautiful stationery or in a frame.

Buy back-to-school supplies for your favorite teacher.

Buy a pretty box and fill it with your friend's favorites: always appreciated are a scented candle, boxed notecards, custom stamps, special pens, and fun stickers.

Fill a basket with living plants: an "English garden" that lasts a long time.

Make a candy necklace; it's so easy and will be treasured by children (although perhaps not by their parents). Using a darning needle and thin fabric ribbon, string the ribbon through the paper "ends" of wrapped candies.

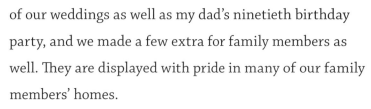

Customize a tray or a box as a memento of a special occasion. We did this for each of our weddings as well as my dad's ninetieth birthday party, and we made a few extra for family members as well. They are displayed with pride in many of our family members' homes.

Make a quilt with an emblem that is meaningful to the recipient (country club, boating flag, horse racing silks, family tree, military insignia); it is a lovely gift and so unique.

Fill an incredibly pretty bowl with beautiful apples (or cherries or oranges).

Fill a great-looking box with all sorts of wrapping paper and supplies.

If a friend is having a birthday later in his or her life, do something incredibly nice. Examples might be sending bingo gifts to his or her retirement home, planting a tree on the grounds of his or her university with a plaque attached, or ordering dinner every Monday night for a month just so your friend doesn't have to cook. There are a hundred other creative ways to say you care.

Plant a pot or window box with bulbs that will soon bloom.

Embroider or print custom clothes for just about any occasion

Give your child's baby clothes to your son or daughter on the birth of their first child— if you have saved everything like I did.

Have an image of just about anything etched onto a block of crystal: use a favorite photo to create a treasure.

Creative Family Photos

My family is a total pain about taking family photos. I really need to get creative to get their buy-in. So, one year for Bobby's birthday, we had everyone coming to our home for dinner. We had recently welcomed the first two babies in our family: Cora, my grandchild, and Bob's grandchild, Joey. I asked our families, as a gift to Bobby, to wear pink if they were my family and blue if they were Bobby's family. Unbeknownst to them, we had a friend come over who is a really good photographer, and he took a family photo. The pictures are precious. TEAM PINK and TEAM BLUE. Our Christmas card announced our new babies and everyone could tell who went with whom. Sometimes just being a little tricky is a good thing.

Framing Memories: Holiday Photo Cards

Many of us are now sending family photo cards for the holidays—and I'll bet you've saved your family's photo cards from previous years. Consider placing them in identical frames and hanging them in chronological order on a focal wall. The look is charming, and so are the memories.

MEMORIES ALIVE

When people you love leave this earth, it is incredibly hard. My mom loved to garden and she especially loved the flower called white alyssum. I plant it in prominent places every spring. It's a gentle reminder, and every time I look at it, I remember that she is always in my heart. It is also special to tell my grandkids that this was my mom's favorite flower. It's just a way to keep the memories alive.

Bobby died when my grandkids were two or under. Yet a couple of them knew "Bob Bob" really well. He would drive them in the golf cart, give them rough-and-tumble horsey rides on his knees, and even when the cancer was getting to him, get on the floor and bark like a dog at these little ones, and they would run away and giggle. We had customized some mugs for Bob for Christmas with photos of him hugging the grandkids. Now I pull out those mugs and serve a cereal treat or little cookies in them, and I remind the kids that these are Bob Bob's special treat mugs. They always get excited (what little kid doesn't get excited for Cap'n Crunch or mini cookies?), and seeing the photos helps to keep Bob Bob alive in their little heads. That is special for all of us.

Embellish the top of the box to make the gift especially cute; consider some of these ideas:

- Silk flowers
- An oversize wrapped Christmas cookie or ornament
- Mittens
- Little toys, cars, paddle and balls, a colorful card with jacks, rag doll
- A baby bib, infant toy, hair ribbons, rattle
- Metal heart
- Measuring spoons
- Large sucker, oversize candy
- A picture frame that holds a special photo
- Gardening tools or seeds

Or just about anything cute you can think of.

Little toys

A metal heart

More seeds!

A Little Out of the Ordinary: Happy Fiftieth

Give fifty gifts for a fiftieth birthday. Throw a party for a friend's "big" birthday and ask every guest to bring that number of something for the birthday girl or guy. The "something" can be things or lists of things—both are equally wonderful. So, on the gift front, think about giving FIFTY of any of these:

- Fancy pencils
- Tennis balls
- Single dollar bills
- Golf balls
- Pieces of their favorite candy
- Individual flowers made into a bouquet
- Favorite paperback books
- Photographs
- Pretty stamps

- Greeting cards
- Rolls of toilet paper
- Bottles of beer
- Cupcakes
- Annuals ready to be planted into a garden
- Apples
- Dog bones for their pup
- Golf tees

And equally fun and maybe even more special are "think-about" lists. Give a list of your favorite FIFTY of any of these:

- Books
- Songs
- Quotes
- Family recipes

- Great things to do
- Reasons you love the birthday person (framed)

Be silly or real; anything is fun!

Portable Pictures

My sweet granddaughter loves to walk around with framed pictures and point out all the people she knows. I made her a laminated set of photos (like flash cards) of all the people she loves. Simply print pictures on paper, make a double-sided card, and laminate it. It's even better if you can get the rounded edges for the laminated cards—or just trim off the sharp corners. They're great to carry to restaurants or on car rides: they're easily wipeable, and there's no dropping of your favorite frames. She loves her "picturs." Thanks to my daughter Lizzy for the idea.

Custom "Painted" Notecards

Do you know the app Waterlogue? If you don't—download it. It paints your photographs. Simply take photos of your home, vacation sights, gardens, your kids or grandkids. When taking photos of people, catching them from the back works better, something like two toddlers holding hands and looking at the beach.

Waterlogue these photos and make them into folded note cards for someone you love—a real treat. Of course, you can do this with regular photographs, but the Waterlogue concept is pretty neat. Shutterfly will make the cards for you.

Custom Albums for Your Kids

Another fun gift idea is to make a photo book of old photos through the years for each of your kids. Mix up the ages of the photos, but give them their own book of photos of themselves throughout their lives. I have done old-fashioned photo albums, or now you can scan the pictures and make a hard-bound book. Either way, it's pretty magical. Having all three of my kids open these gifts on Christmas Eve is very special. One point for the old-fashioned photo albums: I leave about ten pages of photo sleeves so they can add to it.

Embroider It

For the new mom and dad, buy plain cute bibs or soft, cozy receiving blankets—simple ones—and have them embroidered. Make them personal. Use the baby's initials or name, or personalize with a theme or symbol that is important to the family. You can portray a future artist, teacher, or doctor; use a saying that means a lot to you or the family; or make a family tree. There are all kinds of embroidery businesses that will do this for you, or you can try Etsy.com. A week's worth of personalized bibs or receiving blankets is fun to give and fun to receive.

Babies Grow! Shop for the Future

When giving clothes for a new baby, think "older." In other words, so many people give newborns clothes in the tiniest sizes, newborn to three months and three to six months. Those babies are better dressed than they will be at any other time in their lives—but they grow so incredibly quickly. Think about clothing in twelve-month or eighteen-month sizes—even toddler size two. The clothes may seem really big to the new mom and dad when they first see them, but after a few months of growing out of too-small infant clothes, they will be truly grateful. And don't forget to send along a little gift to the sibling. That usually is MOST appreciated.

CHAPTER 08

Bobby's Journey

With thoughts from

James P. Chandler, MD

Lavin/Fates Professor of Neurological Surgery and Surgical Director
Northwestern Brain Tumor Institute

It's been stated that if you want to truly judge an individual's character, look not at how they manage adversity, but how they manage power. I would argue that depending on the nature of the adversity, both are equally important in assessing the depth of one's character. I've had the privilege of knowing Carol Bernick for over four years. During this time I have observed how she manages power in her capacity as the chairman of the board of Northwestern Memorial HealthCare and her many companies, as well as how she managed the love of her life being diagnosed with a malignant brain tumor and their mutual journey towards his death. In my view, her character is quite admirable and beyond reproach.

On the evening of June 29, 2012, I was called by a colleague, Dr. Mary Beth Richmond, to assess a patient of hers, Mr. Bobby Fates, in the emergency room where he presented headaches and had an MRI that showed a tumor in the left temporal area of his brain. When I arrived in the emergency room, Bobby was in bed, his demeanor upbeat, and his mood positive. He was flanked by Carol; his physician of many years, Dr. Richmond; and the CEO of Northwestern Memorial HealthCare, Mr. Dean Harrison. The intensity of the concern on the part of everyone in the room was palpable. When reviewing the MRI of his brain, it was clear that he had a growth, however, the nature of the growth, benign or malignant, was not clear to me. I explained to the group that given the pressure that was being exerted by the growth on the surrounding brain tissue, Bobby would be best served with a surgical resection of the tumor. I further explained that the left temporal lobe had a variety of important functions including speech comprehension, short-term memory, and some components of vision.

Bobby looked me in the eyes and told me to do what we had to do to solve the problem. I saw both a look of confidence and a look of fear as he absorbed the news and realized that this was a situation that was out of his control. I later learned that Bobby was a self-made man who had built several companies from the ground up and had taken care of many people along the way. In his capacity as a leader, fighter, and owner of a major company, he was accustomed to being in control of virtually every aspect of his life. However, health, the most important aspect of one's life, he could not control, and he would have to rely on friends, family, and his care providers. On July 2, 2012, Bobby underwent brain surgery for removal of his tumor.

In surgery, it appeared to me that the lesion had the potential to be aggressive, and as such, I took a fairly aggressive posture removing the tumor, a portion of the surrounding brain tissue, and a portion of the covering of the brain that appeared to be involved. Knowing that every individual's brain is wired slightly differently, I had some concerns as to what the neurologic consequences of the surgery might be. When I went to the recovery room to assess Bobby after the procedure, he was sitting up, wide awake, not speaking. My initial concern was that his language centers had been affected. I asked Bobby if he was okay and if he could speak, to which he responded by looking at me and mimicking his golf swing. He then began to smile and stated, "Yes, I'm fine, doc." What I didn't realize was that Bobby was a passionate golfer, and that golf played a tremendous part in the quality of his life. We were all thrilled that he had done so well with the surgery, however, the pathology did reveal the tumor to be a malignancy called a gliosarcoma. This is a rare tumor, which in the medical literature carries a prognosis, despite all that we do, of death within eight to twelve months.

Bobby was subsequently treated with radiation to the area and then went on to receive chemotherapy. There were several visits that occurred during the course of his treatment, during which he was always accompanied by Carol. Carol assumed the very difficult and challenging role of a companion, care provider, and advocate. At each visit, she carried with her a binder that detailed a journal of Bobby's behavior, his reactions to medication, and all the information directed to her and Bobby by his various care providers. So detailed were her notes that when Bobby was having symptoms that were atypical, or of unclear etiology, her notes, observations, and good judgment ultimately led to identification and appropriate treatment of many of his problems. I recall on several occasions observing Carol effectively manage a variety of emotions that Bobby exhibited during his visits to my office, including fear, uncertainty, and loss of control. While I did my best to put his fears to rest while maintaining a realistic perspective of the situation, Carol allowed him to feel in control and assured him that all would be okay.

Bobby went on to undergo two additional surgeries, and as he approached the three-year anniversary of his original diagnosis, it was clear that his disease was progressing despite our best efforts. Quality of life and maintenance of dignity was of paramount importance to Bobby, Carol, and certainly myself. The time came when we determined that additional treatments were more harmful than helpful. Carol elected to take Bobby home and be his primary caregiver and support. There were, of course, other family members and nursing staff that aided, but it was Carol who was by his side taking him to the bathroom all throughout the evenings, providing his medication, and lying by his side providing him comfort. I called Carol one evening after it was clear that Bobby would not be recovering and was at home transitioning towards death. She explained that he was minimally communicative, not mobile, and for the most part, was confined to the sofa where she and other family members had established all that he needed for care. My nurse and I went to Carol's home to see if there was anything that was needed or that we could do to lessen the burden. Carol was there, on the sofa next to Bobby, caressing him, showing him love and compassion. She was clearly feeling the pain of the moment, but indicated that she was fine and he was fine—and that they were both at peace. She stayed there with Bobby until his passing.

When delivering the news that one has a malignant brain tumor and a limited time to live, it's not too dissimilar to giving a death sentence. As I look into a patient's eyes and into the eyes of their loved ones, I get a glimpse into their soul, and into their character. Having delivered this news many times over the past twenty years, I can tell you that few exhibit the courage and the tenacity that both Carol and Bob exhibited upon hearing their lives would forever be changed. I frequently told Carol that so impressed was I with her advocacy and care of Bobby, that should I ever be sick, she's the person I would want by my side. All too often, facing such intense adversity, patients and their loved ones not surprisingly withdraw. The treatments required in dealing with a complex problem such as brain cancer can be daunting and many times terrifying. Bobby passed on to heaven on February 18, 2016. During this very difficult and dark time in Carol's personal life, she helped navigate Northwestern Memorial HealthCare through a transformative period with sophistication and class, and at no point did she compromise her values, which made her the successful and beloved leader that she has been for many years.

Note: Bobby and my dad wanted to honor Jim and his compassion and care. We wanted to name the Lavin/Fates Chair after Jim but that is not done at Northwestern with active faculty. So, many years in the future when Jim retires from Northwestern, the chair will be renamed the James Chandler Chair. If you ever need a brain surgeon, and I sure hope you don't, I would suggest you look up the credentials of this incredible doctor. You or your family could not be in better or more compassionate hands.

Give thanks.
Always give THANKS.

C.L.B.

Writing about Illness

As I have mentioned several times in this book, I feel I have led a privileged life. Hard work, sure. Careful planning, sure. Ups and downs, sure. But, all in all, it has been a privileged life.

One of the greatest privileges was loving Bobby—the wonderful Bob Fates. He was an amazing man, and I am so grateful he came into my life.

This man was an entrepreneur and an executive. He was a golfer who had won many club championships. He was cute, fun, smart, and funny. All in all, we had eight great years together. In year four, he was diagnosed with brain cancer.

This cancer stuff is mostly awful, but there were wonderful days and memories, and frankly we had many, many wonderful months from the time of the diagnosis until the time we lost him. If I were to guess, I would say that 75 percent of the time we had together from the time of his illness was pretty darn great. He had three operations in total. The last operation was very tough. He lost some of his cognitive function. He could still enjoy life and was an absolute pleasure to be with; I would not change a minute of the time I had with the love of my life. But when brain cancer takes part of your skills or thinking capabilities, it is devastating—especially for the patient. Bobby was super smart and after the last operation, we dealt with all the psychological issues that come with the understanding that the remote control is hard to maneuver, the doctors no longer allow you to drive, and you can't communicate exactly as you did before.

Bobby was a philosophy major in college, and when we talked about his illness, I encouraged him to give our children the memory of his strength and perseverance in how one deals with adversity. He rose to that challenge, and I was amazingly proud of this darling man.

When someone you love is suddenly very sick, it turns your whole world upside down. When Bobby got cancer, I started to write CNN (Carol's news network) to keep friends and family up to date. I had so many people comment on how much my emails helped them that I have tried to recap lessons learned and advice I would give "after the fact." By after the fact I mean I am rereading these now and trying to dissect the lessons. I hope these emails and my advice help someone. It is incredibly hard no matter how one communicates. Here is the beginning of Bobby's story and a few updates from much later in our journey; you'll get a sense of the raw emotions I experienced each step of the way. As I reread all of these, I would tell anyone going through similar issues to take it one day, and sometimes one hour, at a time. And lean on people who care. It helps.

Let your faith be bigger than your fear.

Hebrews 13:6

Choose to be optimistic.
It feels better.

Dalai Lama XIV

June 30, 2012

Hello all you sweet people.

For some of you this is new news: Bob had headaches—certainly not even very bad ones but they lingered for a couple of weeks. CAT scans and MRIs showed a tumor—diagnosed yesterday afternoon.

So this is what we know: Jimmy (Bobby's brother) and I were with Dr. Chandler this morning while he went through next steps. Cancer is not in his body—we know that from the CAT scan. When tumors like this start in the brain at his age they can be fast-growing and they act aggressively. They will do surgery on Monday. Typical Bobby: he asked what his chances of dying from the operation are. Chandler said 1 percent and not from his surgery but the risks of anesthesia.

This tumor is located in the front temporal lobe, which is where speech and memory are—and your golf swing (Bob's humor). The good news is the tumor is the size of a nickel now and Dr. Chandler thinks he can remove it without affecting neurological functions. Of course, he doesn't really know anything until he goes in. The surgery will be about three hours; then he will go to a regular floor and he will stay in the hospital for two to five days. Then it will take a while—several days, three to five? I forget what he said about knowing how long the pathology results will take. In Bobby's age group it is more often cancer—but we could get lucky. There is a small chance it is vascular, and it could be a benign tumor—either of those would be great outcomes. But if it is cancer then we see how much of it our surgeon thinks he took out and then it is up to the oncology folks as to the next form of treatment. (AGAIN: only if they confirm it is cancer.)

So this is scary and we all hate it. Bobby is on steroids and other meds which make him emotional—but 95 percent of the time he is great. Send up a whole bunch of prayers please. They are letting us go home tonight or Sunday and we go back early Monday for the surgery. Northwestern is great at neuro and Dr. Chandler is GREAT. We are eating pizza at home tonight with some family, Bobby's and mine. Hugs to you all. Will email when we know more, Carol

Advice written after the fact

Tell the truth and tell it straight. Give as much of the information as you have. Admit your fears, convince people you have the right doctors so you don't get all kinds of other recommendations if you don't want them. Or if you do want other recommendations, ask for help. Bobby went to the doctor for his headaches way earlier than many men might have. The doctors say this may have saved his life. **Go seek help early.**

Important note: When I sent out these emails, I sent them to myself and blind copied the many people on the list; I didn't want the world to have all the email addresses of folks who had entrusted them to me. That may sound crazy, but there were a few people high up in government who were friends, so just give some thought as to whether you want the world to see your list. Of course, on the other hand, it tells your friends who you have already contacted; so just make your choice after considering both options.

Life is tough, my darling, but so are you.

Stephanie Bennett-Henry

July 2, 2012 at 7:02 PM

Well, he looks good. He is still coming out of the drugs but his speech is normal and his memory is intact but he should get even sharper when all the meds are out of his system. The meds are making him emotional. He is crazy about me right now and I will enjoy that while it lasts! We are all feeling pretty lucky getting through today. We don't know if it is cancer, and we won't know for a week, but the doctor said he took extra tissue because he thought he could without affecting function and was looking for better margins. So, we will pray and we will see. A cute story: Dr. Chandler told us as Bobby was coming out of the anesthesia he was gripping his hands and the doctor asked what he was doing and he said seeing if he remembered how to swing a club!!!! Thanks for your prayers. We have a long way to go but we are thankful for today.

Love,

C

Advice written after the fact

Updates are critical. Try to add a little humor. It helps people know that you are handling the situation as well as can be expected and frankly makes it easier for people to read.

you never know how strong you are until being STRONG is the only choice you have.

Bob Marley

Love is not just about finding a good partner. It's also about being a good one.

Unknown

July 5, 2012 at 10:58 AM

So. Good morning all,

Just came back from getting some bandages removed. I thought they would have the path report but they did not; so any of you sending good thoughts and prayers "upwards," we will ask that you continue to do so. So grateful for your kindness and prayers.

He did well yesterday. We watched a movie (*As Good as It Gets*); I highly recommend you watch that again as it is really cute and fun. His concentration is good sometimes and sometimes not. He is on so many meds right now that a couple of them put him right to sleep. Good news is he didn't want pain meds this a.m. He will be on a couple of drugs for a while; they say that your body will get used to them in a week or so and they taught us new "times of the day" to give the medicine so they are less troublesome. I am reading Bobby all your emails; some make him laugh and that is great. He is overwhelmed with the many people who have expressed concern. I know most of you probably know this, but underneath the somewhat gruff/all-male exterior is one very soft and wonderful human with a huge heart and great values. Your kindness and caring is wonderful.

Bob is allowed to take drives and walk outside (are you kidding me in this heat?) once he gets his energy back. He won't get the staples out for fourteen days; but honestly, he has all his hair and looks pretty darn good. He wore a pink shirt to the doctor (chosen totally by Bobby) so fashion instincts are still totally intact! Black eye is going away pretty quickly. He is telling my dad that he is ready to buy him his special scotch and hopefully will be up and around more in a few days.

I know this is far more than many of you want to know, so just hit delete when you see the CNN update. But it is just easier to communicate with so many people who have expressed concern. I will write when there is more to tell. Hugs to all of you. So grateful. C

Advice written after the fact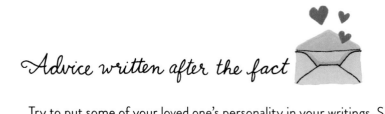

Try to put some of your loved one's personality in your writings. Show normalcy when you are lucky enough to have some. Bobby's and my friends needed comfort too. A whole lot of us were hurting watching him go through all of this and it's a kindness to tell your audience that he is still himself—funny, irreverent, smart, a little bit of a fashion hound, and a heck of an athlete.

Day by Day

●●●●●●●●●●●●●●●

John-Michael Tebelak, *Godspell*

July 6, 2012 at 8:08 AM

Good morning friends and family,

This morning is a whole lot better than yesterday—yea! He is able to watch the news and concentrate. He just called Michael to tell him something about the stock market. Yesterday was a little scary. He was so exhausted and felt awful—could not really keep him up much and a real downturn from the day before. Grouchy too! Anyway, the docs told me to expect a roller coaster so I had four cocktails and held on. (That's a joke for the folks who don't know me; I infrequently drink wine. But if you hide that liquor in a frozen daiquiri and serve it on a beach in the Bahamas—well, that is a little different.)

For whatever reason, last night about 8:30 p.m. I decided to take all my hand-written medical notes on Bobby and put them in my computer so we would have a record for reference, and I read one note that I had written on his discharge (one note on 6 pages of info). The note said contact the office if he gets excessively tired, nauseous, or has speech or focus issues. OMG was that was what I was dealing with? I freaked of course and called the office which, of course, is closed. The guy who answers says, "Well, is

*I can't promise to fix all your problems
but I can promise
you won't have to face them alone.*

. . . .
Anonymous

this an emergency?" and I say no; so he says call back tomorrow. So I say, okay, it IS an emergency maybe so get me a neuro resident or someone to call me back. They call and tell me to come to the emergency room...and I call Mary Beth Richmond, our unbelievably wonderful internist, and she says GO. She even recommends an ambulance and now I am really freaking. Bob of course does not want to go. I called Lizzy and Dan (my daughter and son-in-law) to come over to get us as they live so close and I knew they were home so we went by car. JUST GLAD WE DID. He had a CAT scan and was fine, and that alone makes you feel so much better. Turns out some people "come off" steroids differently and they think he was reacting to the lesser dose. They put him back on a higher dose of steroids, sent us home, and this morning he is MUCH better. He has been listening to the news for 2 hours and this is the first time, to quote Bobby, that "he has been cognizant." YEA!!! I love Bob's mind and we talk all the time about real issues; so I can't wait for him to get back to his old self and this morning feels SO much better. We are not home free by any means, but certainly a good beginning.

So now four of you "friends" have written that you want to play golf with Bobby now—like right now—because you think it's the only time you can BEAT HIM! Fair warning: the steroids just might make those drives even longer!

And from my "sweet" father, see his note below!

> *Hi Bob,*
> *I am so pleased to hear that you are doing so well! Now that you have your memory*
> *back, I hope you remember 3 weeks ago I loaned you $5,000.00. Please remember*
> *fast pay makes fast friends. I look forward to seeing your smiling face very soon.*
> *My thoughts for good health are always with you!*
> *Leonard*

And NO, there was never a loan! (My dad is still very with it at 93.)

So do you remember that the nurse yesterday told him to get outside and take a walk? I

Focus on the *good.*

Unknown

got a real kick out of Marty Whealy's mom who was a nurse a long time ago; here is her cute response to that!

> *GO AGAINST MEDICAL ADVICE! Who is the idiot who told him to walk outside in 102-degree heat? Sorry, Nurse Shirley had to have her say. Maybe Lake Shore Drive is 72 degrees. "Cooler near the lake?" Oh, sure.*

THANKS SHIRLEY! THAT HAD ME SMILING.

So he is counting down the seconds to the jobs report; that is great! And watching the news next to me as I write this.

Many of you have asked to visit. Frankly, Bobby is just not ready to see folks. He just doesn't want to yet. Maybe today will turn that, as he is more focused. He really looks pretty good. Of course he sees his kids and Jimmy and my kids and everyone keeps bringing him food! So, a word about food: Bobby is usually pretty good about eating more healthily than not but all this boy wants now is Portillo's hot dogs, griddle cake breakfasts from McDonald's, and cheese popcorn from Garrett's! ENOUGH. Nurse Carol will force-feed some fruit into this guy if it kills me. Thanks to all our family who keep indulging him. Next time bring lettuce!

So many of you have sent my notes on to folks who I don't know well or have not met. Thanks to you all for caring and for all your prayers and kindness. I look forward to meeting all the people I don't know. Thanks for caring about our Bobby. Keep the prayers coming. I am sure we are where we are because of all your love and prayers.

Stay cool! Lots of hugs, Carol and of course Bobby!

An act of kindness, when wrapped in love, is often the ingredient that creates miracles for others.

Mary Ellen

*Today is a good day
to have a good day.*

Unknown

And from my college friend Chuck O'Brien, who is a physician. I left out the medical help Chuck offered (it is a godsend to have all the docs we know help us get through this); but I left in Chuck's form of humor!

> *Doing so well so early is awesome. Tell Bob that either the surgeon was great or he didn't have any normal brain tissue to damage!!!! He can decide.*
> *Give him my best. Chuck*

So to all you wonderful people: we think they will get the path report next week, early, I would assume, and of course we are on pins and needles about that but we are in great hands and the results to date have been awesome. To think you can be diagnosed on Friday, have surgery on Monday, be home on Tuesday night (that still has me shaking my head!), and go from being so sleepy you can't open your eyes one day to trying on your wardrobe the next! Well, life is a wild ride and we have been so lucky to have so many wonderful people in our lives to share the journey. Thank you. We feel most blessed today. And I think we will actually go OUTSIDE FOR A WALK!

Love to you all! "Light and love and laughter"—and friends! Carol and Bobby

Quote of the day from my friend Mary: "Courage is fear that has said its prayers."

Advice written after the fact

There will be great days. Enjoy them. Celebrate every normal thing that comes your way. This is an incredibly hard journey and you will learn something every day. Good people like to help and they often don't know what to do. Help them to help you laugh. It is a good thing.

July 11, 2012 at 5:50 PM

So, a very long day—and a wonderful day. We went to Medinah and watched Kate take a great golf lesson; we loved every minute of it. And then we waited.

Bobby does have cancer. It is an extremely rare form of cancer. Something like eleven cases EVER reported in the literature—not in the USA but anywhere. It is called malignant spindle cell neoplasm. Mary Beth (our fantastic internist and a previous chief of staff at Northwestern Memorial) told us the last time she ever heard those words was in medical school—and not related to brain cancer. Anyway, the reason the path report has taken so long is that Dr. Chandler and Dr. Mehta sent the path report to Memorial Sloan Kettering for a second opinion; BUT neither Memorial Sloan nor MD Anderson will have had very many cases, if any. So, Dr. Chandler looks at us and says he feels very, very good about the outcome. They will pow-wow with their colleagues from other top cancer centers but they are leaning toward a one-day, six-hour procedure of radiation with the gamma knife. Dr. Chandler will do this: it is pinpointed radiation. A long procedure but one day and he goes home. They don't expect side effects from this. And then we would be done with radiation. They feel this has the best chance of delivering the most concentrated dose and IF there were cancer cells left, that this would get at them. The other standard form of radiation is something like six weeks every day. They feel that by doing the one-day procedure, if the cancer does come back they could always do the standard radiation later. Dr. Chandler thought when he first operated that Bobby had the "Ted Kennedy" kind of cancer (a glioblastoma), which takes your life very quickly; and because of that he went after much bigger margins. When Dr. Chandler came out of the surgery he did not think it was the Kennedy kind of cancer but it was hugely fortuitous that he took the extra margin, especially since it turned out to be what it was.

You must do the thing you think you cannot do.

Eleanor Roosevelt

I don't need easy,
I just need possible.

Bethany Hamilton, *Soul Surfer*

Bobby can drive in a week, putt NOW, golf in 4 weeks from the surgery, have half of a Captain Morgan and Diet Coke now if he wants it—but the doctors would suggest we stick to straight Diet Cokes for a week. Staples come out next week. He has three more MRIs just to rule out any spine involvement—which they do not expect. If something came up there, we would be back to the drawing board. Depending on the second pathology opinion there is a chance he might have oral chemo for a while—but that is not bad at all. So, they will check him every so often once this all is done. But the doctors feel GOOD and we feel so thankful. I am POSITIVE ALL PRAYERS AND GOOD THOUGHTS HELPED. We are the luckiest people in the world to have so many people care. We are so incredibly fortunate to have had Dr. Chandler and Dr. Mehta, who is one of the best radiation oncologists around. I am so proud to be associated with this incredible institution and will brag in a few days about the latest US News and World Report ratings, which I can't brag about now, as they are not yet released—but I have copied Dean Harrison on this and could not feel any more grateful to the docs and the hospital than I do now. I don't know if you all know this, but my "love affair" with NMHC (Northwestern Memorial HealthCare) started thirty years ago when my son Peter was born. I had high-risk pregnancies (Craig was born seven weeks early and we lost a baby that was stillborn after seven months) and I have worked hard to help that institution for years. Watch out, Dean: how much more grateful can one family get!

So, we have work to do, and we will do it. It is cancer and it is serious. But the outcome is pretty darn good, and we are smiling. Love you all. Thanks for everything. I will not likely keep up the CNN (Carol news network) as I am sure you have had enough; but once we get to the final treatment plans I will let you know. And, of course, if anything changes you will hear from us. Bobby is recovering nicely from the operation and I am sure he will be seeing many of you SOON! Might even take a cart around Big Foot this weekend.

Thanks to all of you from the bottom of our hearts. With much love, Carol and Bob

Advice written after the fact

The great institutions like Northwestern Memorial Hospital ask other great hospitals for second opinions. Bobby's cancer was not like anything they had seen so they went outside to their incredibly good networks and asked others to verify or challenge their opinions.

Cancer is a hard disease to fight. Staying positive is hugely important. I will share with you something a friend sent to me. It is something I reread often. It is definitely a lesson. This is from Carolyn Smith, a friend in Texas. She is the lady that married my college friend Kent (read that as my college boyfriend!), who passed away just before Bobby's surgery after having been diagnosed with ALS.

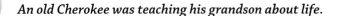

An old Cherokee was teaching his grandson about life.

"A fight is going on inside me," he said to the boy. "It is a terrible fight and it's between two wolves. One wolf is evil: he is anger, envy, sorrow, regret, greed, arrogance, self-pity, guilt, resentment, inferiority, lies, false pride, superiority, and ego." He continued, "The other is a good wolf: he is joy, peace, love, hope, serenity, humility, kindness, benevolence, empathy, generosity, truth, compassion, and faith. The same fight is going on inside you," he told his grandson, "and inside every other person, too."

The grandson thought about it for a minute and then asked his grandfather, "Which wolf will win?"

The old Cherokee simply replied, "The one you feed."

When you are down to nothing
God is up to something.

Proverbs 16:9

July 23, 2012 at 9:24 PM

Hi all,

I have answered the phone multiple times tonight and have eight emails already wondering about Bobby, so I will fill you ALL in on where we are as of our 1 p.m. meeting with all the docs today. We were to have met with them last Thursday but the appointment was canceled as they were still doing more pathology testing. We spent a good part of today learning all that we needed to know. We are good—truly. We are overwhelmed by the "process" and the caring and the incredible talent that is surrounding us and the fact of having a lot to learn and a lot to deal with. The overall news is Dr. Chandler and Dr. Mehta feel very good about Bob's chances. This is a different kind of cancer than previously believed—"we think." Memorial Sloan Kettering took quite a long time because they too requested a bunch more stains; and even after all the experts have weighed in we have what is called a "soft" diagnosis. They DO believe now that the cancer did in fact begin in and around the brain and that is unusual. This cancer is rare but less rare than the original diagnosis. They are calling the tumor a gliosarcoma. They said they see elements of a gliosarcoma but can't call it that categorically; and if we read all the literature about gliosarcomas, a lot of what we read would not apply to Bob's tumor. I am editing comments here from about six conversations with different docs and specialists.

Treatment
Combination: gamma-knife radiation followed by standard external fractional beam radiation with oral chemotherapy.

This is an aggressive kind of cancer and can come back right where it started. Currently all MRIs show a normal brain.

Because of where the cancer is, in the front part of the cavity, it can take a substantially higher dose of radiation and all the experts feel that we can be aggressive with treatment and that is the best way to go. Many tumors cannot take gamma-knife radiation due to their location. This will now be followed with daily radiation for thirty treatments. It takes twenty minutes every day for thirty days. No pain—pretty simple, they say. Bobby will take an oral chemotherapy pill with the daily radiation. They believe the oral chemotherapy makes the radiation work better. The pill can make you tired; some people experience nausea but they give you meds for this and most people go about their daily lives and function just fine.

Once the radiation is done, you take a month-long break and let the body recover. Then it's five days of oral chemo and twenty-three days off. This continues for usually six months but some places suggest it for a year; they will call this later. They will do scans every six weeks.

The good news is the side effects are usually not too tough from oral chemo. It is not like the IV kind. Both Chandler and Mehta talked about this protocol having been developed with a collection of the brightest minds around the country. And again, they feel positive.

So, the gamma-knife radiation is the day after tomorrow. And the standard radiation starts next Monday. They say he will be just fine but might want to rest up on Thursday.

A comment about the best and the brightest. I see this all the time in business. The smartest people I know ask for help. They seek out other opinions and "egos get left at the door" and it is wonderful to see. Our team is fantastic; we have total confidence in them and we are grateful they reached out to other world-class experts to confirm next steps. Many of you have offered up people and places and contacts. We are grateful. Frankly we know the top folks at MD Anderson and at the Cleveland Clinic, and dear friends have great contacts at Duke and Mayo. We are grateful for all the suggestions and help. But truly both Bobby and I and his family are very comfortable we have great docs, have confirmed the diagnosis with a second opinion from more top experts, and are in great hands.

To all you doctors in the email list: forgive me, I am sure some of this is wrong; but hopefully the "gist" is on target. Kinda overwhelming to us shampoo folk!

A couple of interesting things. They said: don't use any antioxidant pills or supplements of any kind, even natural ones. Limit sugar. Be positive, live your life; go to work, do functional things. And when I asked our doc if we should read all the books that were being given to us (even by their staff) he looked at us and smiled and said "NO"; a lot of what we would read doesn't apply to us. People will start reading up on Bob's kind of tumor and most of it will be wrong, as his does not present as seen in the literature. We are in great hands, so we will stay strong, eat well, visit their group that deals with nutrition and alternative therapies, and know that we have GREAT care.

About Mr. Bob

So Bobby has been walking two-plus miles, working at his office most of the day. He has been enjoying a few friends and a lot of family. We have been told he can travel (over the weekends; just be back for the treatments for the next couple of weeks). We will be able to travel to Florida this winter and frankly should be able to live life as normal. He spends a whole bunch of time trying on clothes!!! He needs to get rid of half of these, as he had three sizes and now they all fit and he wants more closet space and THAT simply is NOT going to happen! We are playing, walking; he is able to drive now AND WILL BE ABLE TO START HITTING golf balls next week. If he reacts well to that, he will be able to play eighteen holes soon. And we look forward to entertaining a bunch of you in the coming weeks!

We have options, and we have a plan. We have the best physicians out there. We have fantastic family and friends. We feel so fortunate that we have a path that people think gives him a very good chance; and we will get through this and he will probably improve his golf swing in the process.

We believe strongly the prayers are working; we ask that you keep them coming. Thanks for caring, and know that you mean the world to us. With many hugs to you all.

Carol and Bob

Advice written after the fact

Life can be tough. Pick yourself up, dust off your jeans, and move forward. Prayer does help. Staying positive helps. The diagnosis changed from medium-okay to more complicated but still hopeful. Hopeful is a very good thing. I was chairman of this amazing hospital system at the time of Bobby's diagnosis and I am positive our care and our doctors are as good as it gets. Not everyone has the access we had. I work my rear off to connect people I know to the great folks I have had the privilege to get to know over the almost twenty years I have "worked for" Northwestern Memorial HealthCare. Find a great doctor now. If you don't have one, get one. Make sure you understand where your doctor has privileges and make sure you understand how well that hospital does on performance measures. Second opinions are a great thing. If your providers are not looking for confirmation of their thinking, you may want to. With cancer, the path is changing every month and progress is being made.

When life knocks you down, roll over and look at the stars.

Unknown

As part of my diet I'm golfing every day.
My doctor told me to live on
GREENS as much as possible.

Unknown

September 13, 2012 at 10:08 AM

Subject: TODAY'S A GREAT DAY!

RADIATION IS OVER! AND WE ARE CELEBRATING!

SO, HE LOOKS GOOD, HE IS IN A GOOD MOOD, AND WE ARE MOVING FORWARD! BOBBY'S BLOOD COUNTS ARE STILL LOW AND THEY GAVE HIM A SHOT TO BRING UP THE WHITE BLOOD CELL COUNT. THIS WILL MAKE HIM LESS SUSCEPTIBLE TO INFECTION. THEY SAY THAT HIS ENERGY SHOULD COME BACK SLOWLY OVER THE NEXT COUPLE OF WEEKS, SO HE SHOULD STOP BEING THE GOLF COACH AND START BEING THE EIGHTEEN-HOLE PLAYER!!!! HE IS OFF EVERYTHING (CHEMO AND RADIATION) UNTIL ABOUT A MONTH FROM NOW. HE WILL GET AN MRI SCAN IN MID OCTOBER; THAT IS THE "NEW BASELINE" SCAN AND WE GO FROM THERE. HE WILL BE ON ORAL CHEMO FOR FIVE DAYS A MONTH AND OFF FOR TWENTY-FIVE DAYS AND THEN BACK ON; THEY SAY MOST PEOPLE TOLERATE THAT PRETTY WELL. OUR SPIRITS ARE GREAT; HE CAN'T WAIT TO GET BACK TO "FULL TIME LIFE" (ME TOO! ME TOO!) AND WE ARE SO GRATEFUL FOR ALL YOUR EMAILS, CARDS, PRAYERS, AND GOOD THOUGHTS. WISHING YOU A GREAT DAY! CAROL AND BOB!

Advice written after the fact

Always share the positives. People will start breathing again. That's a very good thing. In this journey, there will be great days. Hope is a wonderful thing.

Note: **I have skipped ahead twenty months; this would have been an even longer book if I hadn't! But let me first say that MRIs happened every eight weeks and with them came fear and then rejoicing. He did get back to golfing and was better than ever. Most days were pretty darn good—more fatigue, but we all adjusted.**

May 7, 2014 at 8:43 PM

Hi all,

Well, I know some of you have heard and others have called. Yes, Bobby is scheduled for surgery this Friday. He has had MRIs every two months since the cancer was diagnosed and the last two MRIs have shown some change. Three weeks ago, they put him on steroids and gave us a fifty-fifty chance the change was scar tissue or a regrowth of the tumor. Today the decision was made to operate, as the steroids did not eliminate the chance that it could be cancer. Jim Chandler, Bob's neurosurgeon (fantastic surgeon and now great friend), believes there is a greater chance that it is scar tissue and dead cancer cells but, of course, no one knows until the biopsy is done and the labs come back. So, Bobby is scheduled for surgery on Friday and we will know what we are facing this weekend. It is brain surgery; it is a three-hour operation either way. Luckily Jim thinks it is in a place where no damage will be done. If it is cancer they will likely re-treat him with chemotherapy. Jim is hopeful that the recovery is easier this time, as Bobby's system has tolerated the drugs before, etc. So say a prayer. Either way, our Bobby hopes to be back golfing within the month. Take care and thanks for your love and friendship.

Carol and Bobby

You are stronger than you know... braver than you think...and more loved than you can imagine.

A.A. Milne, *Winnie the Pooh*

Note: Bobby had surgery on May 9, 2014. I had let everyone know; here is the CNN email with the results.

May 16, 2014 at 12:01 PM

You all have been wonderful with your emails and notes. Thank you! We just heard that the recommendation of Northwestern's tumor review board is continued observation and no chemo! This is huge news, of course. The tissue samples that were removed showed scar tissue from the radiation and dead cancer cells—NO ACTIVE/LIVE CANCER CELLS. **We are hugely relieved and thank you all for your prayers and wonderful thoughts.**

They will continue to do MRIs every eight weeks; but so far so good. He is getting stronger each day. The surgery was about three-plus hours and he has to recover from all that; we see Dr. Chandler on Monday. Once again, I cannot say enough about the fantastic team at NMH, led by Jim Chandler.

So, Bobby thought he could hit chip shots using whiffle balls (AGAINST OUR WALLPAPER in the exercise room!) but that was shot down by the great Dr. C. He is still on a bunch of medications that we hope the docs will begin to taper. At the time of surgery they said no golf for three weeks; but my guess is my cute man will negotiate that time down a little.

I enclose two precious pictures. The first one is of Cora, my granddaughter. The note says, "Bears and Prayers...for Geebs." Geebs is, of course, Bobby. GB is short for Grandpa Bob; my daughter, Lizzy, turned that into Geebs. So, we are CC and Geebs. Those bear PJs are Cora's lucky pajamas. She wore them the first time we were babysitting her for the weekend and we won a major horse race that day; so we call them her lucky PJs.

For with God nothing shall be impossible.

Luke 1:37

The second picture is Bobby on the floor with Cora and Joey, who is Bob's grandson. Maybe not the smartest place for Bobby to be after surgery, but it was sure great medicine!

No more CNN updates, hopefully, for a long time. Instead you will see him up and around and hitting those little white balls and back to the office. Feel free to call him; he is up and around and happy to talk. Thanks; our greatest gift is our family and friends. WE ARE SO INCREDIBLY BLESSED; so grateful to you all. Hugs and full of hope, Carol and Bob

Oh, my friend, it's not what they
take away from you that counts,
it's what you do with what you have left.

·····················

Hubert H. Humphrey

So many emails
are missing from our
journey. I close with my
loving thoughts on
Bobby's passing. Bobby was
diagnosed in late June 2012
and left this earth in
February 2016.

One lesson,
I didn't want to learn

·····················

C.L.B.

MY FRIEND MARTY

When I asked one person in my office if I should include a specific photo of Bobby in the chapter on "Bobby's Journey," she said no. I asked my friend Marty the same question and she gave an emphatic YES and sent the following response. I share it because, for any of you going through something like this, it is so true: life goes on. With an ill family member or friend, some days are sweet, some are funny, and some are just very hard. I share this because Bobby truly "lived" right up to the end. It was a gift to all of us.

Bob wasn't confined to a bed or chair, unreachable for four years. Life went on with him and around him, and it is important to show, and for others to see, that it didn't matter to Cora or Joe or Scotty—love is love, and whether he has staples in his head or can't move his arm, it didn't matter to those grandkids—they adored him and crawled right up to be with him and, in some cases, on him.

Bob Bob's couch is epic. Joe in bed with him. Cora in her lucky bear PJ's. Bob singing in the Naples apartment with his lifelong friends. Dr. Chandler arriving at the holiday party, announcing great test results and lifting a bottle of champagne. Bob asking anyone standing in the kitchen while he drank his morning green (awful) cocktail if they wanted to join him! The empty cup on top of the car—remember, he was off to golf! He was Mr. Bickerson late into his last year (Bobby liked to debate you on just about anything). There were casino nights of shared driving—"You just rest in the backseat, Bob. Marty will drive"—our way of NOT having him drive!!! Pictures are life and can show the good, the bad, the ugly, the humor, and the sadness. How 'bout when he sent me that photo of his radiation mask? Really?

Saying Goodbye
to a Loved One

Farewell to Bobby, Eulogy, February 2016

How do I tell you all about this man I loved? He was so much deeper in private than in public. He was incredibly kind and believed in doing the right thing. He was fun, joyful, and loving. He was constantly reading, and he was very smart. And, yes, Lizzy, he could even use tools—sort of. Since Bobby came into our lives we have three new built-in bars (and all the kids thank you for always keeping those bars well stocked and for all the new TVs you added to our world. Really BIG ones!).

*When you can't
look on the bright side
I will sit with you
in the dark.*

••••••••••••••••••••

Lewis Carroll, *Alice's Adventures in Wonderland*

Bobby was my biggest fan. I thank you, Bob, for always having my back. He made me feel special, and he came into my life at a time when I was pretty broken. And come on, guys, to some people, I am told, I am kind of a challenge. But he loved my business life and was a huge supporter: we shared the family value of *hard* work.

One of the very best things I loved about Bobby was his willingness to grow and change—**not that you knew it was going to happen**. For instance, I remember him ripping on someone on the phone, really tough, and when he hung up I asked, "So how did that work for you? Did you achieve what you wanted?" And he just glared. But the next day he would ask me how I would have handled it and, sure enough, he would take that lesson in, and you would see some change. It happened all the time. I thought I was talking to a deaf wall one day and darned if he didn't come back a day or two later and want to talk about whatever the issue was. I told my friends that maybe it was his philosophy degree. For Bobby, lifelong learning was very real.

No one ever could help him. He was more independent than anyone I knew. But in the last several months, he needed Team Bobby: he looked at me and submitted with grace. Over these many years, he came to love his docs. I am positive Bobby had a couple of bonus years—really good years—a true gift from Jim Chandler, our world-class neurosurgeon, and his team. The life span after diagnosis of a gliosarcoma, I am now told, is about eleven months. We had close to four years and I wouldn't trade a day of it. Our thanks to Dr. Priya Kumthekar and her team and to Dr. Mary Beth Richmond, who was with us the entire the time. These incredible docs became our friends—true buddies. So, it should not have surprised me when, about seven months ago, I got a call from Jim Chandler at work. Now you have to know our appointments with this incredible neurosurgeon are scheduled long in advance, and I am there for each one. So when he said Bobby was with him in his office, I freaked. "Jim, what's wrong?" And Jim said, "Well, Bobby walked over to see me because his foot hurt!!! So, I am setting him up with my friend the podiatrist next door. We're sending him over there now." Really????

And I want to thank Team Carol. There are so many of you who had my back from the first diagnosis. Thank you, Marty, and so many others in my life. And thanks to Jim and Sue, Bobby's brother and sister-in-law, who were there any time I needed help and support. They were fantastic and, of course, they loved Bobby as much as I did. It was really wonderful to have that support.

How funny is it that, when Bobby and I first met, for the first month, maybe even two, I had no idea he was a golfer. Bobby was in his total selling mode. He was a fantastic salesman, and I mean fantastic—relentless until he got the sale. Come on now, no golf or sports on the TV ever for as long as two months? He was too busy sending me sixteen emails a day.

On our third date my suave guy took me to buy a computer—a pink computer—because my office email was overheating. And guess what. We ran out of gas.

I had never run out of gas before. It was another first. My suave Bob.

Yes, Jimmy, it was that Mercedes with the broken gas gauge. But Bobby made that fun, too. We got so close incredibly fast. Bob and I met in late September 2007. My mom died a month later, and we had many close calls in that month. Bobby was with me and my family through it all and got to know everyone in my life in an intimate way in about six weeks. From then on, he was part of my family; everyone knew we had something that would last. Bobby was compassionate and loving, and he dropped everything to help us at that very sad time.

The one thing I will not miss is Bobby's driving. He was awful. His family knew I had some influence on Bobby and they wanted me to fix his driving. Impossible. Awful, impossible—and the only time Bobby and I really fought. Bobby did most things in life FAST.

Knowing when to walk away is wisdom. Being willing is courage. Walking away with your head held high is dignity.

• • • • • • • • • • • • • • • •

Sallie Felton

In loving memory of

Robert Henry Fates

September 7, 1946 ~ February 18, 2016

Life is like a round of golf

With many a turn and twist
But the game is much too sweet and short
To curse the shots you've missed.

Sometimes you'll hit it straight and far
Sometimes the putts roll true.
But each round has its errant shots
And troubles to play through.

So always swing with courage
No matter what the lie.
And never let the hazards
Destroy the joy inside.

And keep a song within your heart
Give thanks that you can play.
For the round is much too short and sweet
To let it slip away.

I'd like the memory of me
to be a happy one,
I'd like to leave an afterglow
of smiles when life is done.
I'd like to leave an echo
whispering softly down the ways,
of happy times and laughing times
and bright and sunny days.
I'd like the tears of those who grieve
to dry before the sun
of happy memories
that I leave when life is done.

~ All Are Welcome ~
Memorial Service and Luncheon
Tuesday, February 23, 2016
12:30 PM
Medinah Country Club
6N001 Medinah Road
Medinah, Illinois 60157

Additional Lessons Learned from Illness

So here are some more lessons from Bobby and me, and I hope they will one day help someone you care about—or on second thought, I truly hope you don't experience any of this ever.

Courage does not always roar. Sometimes courage is the quiet voice at the end of the day saying "I will try again tomorrow".

Mary Anne Radmacher

- I said it earlier in a CNN piece, but I advise that you not read all the stuff about an illness. This is so atypical for me, as I always learn everything I can about whatever comes into my life. But with Bobby's diagnosis, we were in great hands; I knew the Northwestern Memorial Hospital team would give us outstanding care, and I didn't need to be scared any more than I already was. As it turned out, some of our great doctors to this day are not sure exactly what kind of cancer Bobby had. Certainly, it was brain cancer, and certainly, it was stage four (but I didn't know that for the first couple of years, and I am so glad I did not; no one mentioned it, and I didn't ask). The "standard" life span for a gliosarcoma is less than a year. If I had known that, I would have been watching for "bad signs" all the time, and I am so glad I didn't read those books. It was so much easier to stay positive just doing what we had to do to try to get Bobby better. I know this piece of advice won't make sense for a lot of you, but if I had to do it all over again, I stand by our actions.

- Radiation can cause necrosis over time. It's a great tool in the beginning, but like any scar tissue, which is what it is, necrosis can infringe on parts of your brain, and you can lose function. For Bobby, we had to watch out for issues like short-term memory and the loss of some language. Bobby had aphasia in the last year of his illness. He would know the word but couldn't say it. Speech therapy can help some, but for us, only some. Doctors can counter necrosis with steroids or chemo in bad cases, but either way, it is something to be aware of.

- Bobby ended up having three surgeries over the three and a half years that he lived. The first, of course, was the removal of his tumor. You are always concerned that the cancer is growing back. MRIs every eight weeks keep you on edge almost always. We found the best way to deal with this fear was to celebrate a lot after a good MRI and not let it scare us until week seven was over. For the most part it worked. The second operation was in May 2014, almost two years after his diagnosis. The results: scar tissue, no live cancer cells. The third operation was in April 2015. The results: a lot of scar tissue and some cancer cells.

- We tried clinical trials. I will tell you that some of them are amazing, but the fact is most of them don't work. But, of course, you try. Just make sure you know the side effects and understand which are long-term and which are temporary. It helps prepare you for what will come.

People don't always need advice. Sometimes all they need is a hand to hold, an ear to listen and a heart to understand them.

Unknown

- Build a support team. You can't do this alone. Bring in friends or family so you can continue to live your life. For me that meant going to work (shorter days for sure) and keeping up those friendships closest to me (occasionally), while every late afternoon and evening were spent with Bobby. People are really kind. Be specific in what you need, and usually they will help. But different people deal with illness in different ways. Some of Bobby's family members just couldn't handle his being sick, and they stayed away more often than we wanted. But our neurosurgeon told me in his experience some people just can't handle the illness of a loved one, and he encouraged me to give them a pass. I wanted what I thought was best for Bobby and that was to have those he loved around him as much as possible. That caused some strain, but over time we made it work. Bobby and his brother were always close but during the time of Bobby's illness, it was special to watch these guys. Take the good that comes with the bad. Cherish it. And give people you love a pass.

- During his illness, Bobby grew even closer to my family. He and my dad were good friends, and they became even more so after Bobby got sick, as my dad was so proud of how he was handling it. Some relationships will become even stronger, and that is a blessing.

- Doctors try to help you. Sometimes they just cannot. If you have a problem, they want to fix it. And sometimes they try things hoping it might make a difference. Sometimes you have to question how much of that you think is smart. For us, we knew that Bobby reacted to medicines in a way that was far different than most people. He "over-reacted"; so for us to add new meds when it wasn't essential was just not something we wanted to do. And I was the one who had to convince the doctors of that until they came to know him really well.

- If you have to go to the emergency room, here's a fact you should know: those coming in by ambulance are seen first. Of course, you don't want to abuse that, but when needed, use the ambulance.

- The doctors will offer other types of help as well: massages, all kinds of therapy (physical, psychological, speech), acupuncture, and more. Try it. Different things work for different people. Bobby was not a "touchy-feely" kind of guy, but he was willing to try almost anything with my pushing. Some of it really helped.

- Steroids are amazing drugs, and they are also simply awful. The agitation and aggression

have just lost the person you love. Okay; I got through that. And, of course, I was thrilled for the bride and groom, truly thrilled. It just brought to the front of my mind again how very much I missed Bobby. The cocktail party was fine, but dinner was very hard. I was sitting at a table of honor with big-time CEOs. They were nice people, but I was more than uncomfortable being alone at this table with folks I didn't really know, with couples conversing and dancing. I learned that the next time I was invited to a formal occasion, I needed to tell my host and hostess that I would really prefer to sit with family or friends. The advice, of course, is to be kind to yourself. And sometimes it is just FINE to take a pass on an event. Grieving is hard stuff, and finding your way again is not always so easy.

I have found that the craziness of my six grandkids is good medicine. "Of course," you would say, but what I mean is that being in very busy situations is a good thing for me. I may yearn for a little peace, but I am sure not lonely. And these crazy monkeys of mine are the cutest things in the world. But I am also careful to not overstay my welcome and not depend too much on my children for emotional support. I don't want my wonderful kids to worry about me, and I don't want to ever be a burden on them.

I go to the office most days, and that is a wonderful thing for me. I like what I do, and I love my team. My days are full of interesting things to do and wonderful people with whom I get to work. My advice to others is to fill your days with very positive and meaningful activities. I have to watch out for weekends. I have been so crazy busy taking care of Bobby that I now need to think a little bit and make plans for the weekends. I have a ton of friends, and I have the ability to run away for the weekend or invite a group to dinner. I used to love to do all that. I just have to work the plan a little. Most of my friends and family are used to me being busy; so on weekends, anyway, it has usually been up to me to connect. I guess it's time to put myself out there.

Another thing I learned right after my separation from my then-husband (when it was a very difficult time in my life) was how much I enjoyed running away with all my best buddies. We spent a wonderful almost full week in Florida and everyone came. I would suggest that you not use up all your best buddies at one time. Spreading out all the caring love that came from my best girlfriends in the world just would have been a better thing. They came from all over to be with me in Florida and, gosh, in hindsight, as wonderful as that week was, it would have been healthier for me to have visited with each of them separately and felt that love over many months of one-on-one trips.

I can't believe how insensitive some people can be. I have been told it is time to start dating again. That happened just a few months after I lost Bobby. Really? It was so hard to hold my tongue. If and when I ever "start dating" (ugh—dating sounds like high school), it will be 100 percent up to me. My advice: don't push people who have lost someone they love. It is very hard the first year. Let them heal.

And finally: for me it is good to spend time with people who really knew the person I loved, whether it was my mom, my brother, or my sweet Bobby. They can laugh and cry with me. And that just feels better.

Life goes on. It can be very hard sometimes. But I am totally a glass-half-full kind of person, and I will take joy in all the other wonderful people and opportunities that life gives to me. I will move forward with joy in my heart and joy in my step. I don't want to miss out on "what's next."

This is the day the Lord has made; let us rejoice and be glad in it.

Psalm 118:24

CHAPTER 09

Above All Else...Family

I had a lot of discussions with myself about the placement of the chapter about family within the book. Without question, in my world, family comes first. And everyone would say "of course"...it does for almost everyone. And I sure hope that is true. But it seemed fitting to place it at the end of the book once folks understood the "all else" in my life. So, I close this book with "Above All Else...Family." To me, families provide a safe haven to be the real you—a place where you can feel loved and treasured regardless of your fears, mistakes, and vulnerabilities. A place where those you cherish are celebrated for their unique qualities, nurtured and grown. A place where boundaries provide the safe borders for a world that can be a little too scary.

As you read through the many wisdoms and life lessons in this chapter, you will come to know my family even more personally. You may come to know them through teenage escapades or via a childhood prank. And you may come to understand some things that almost broke our hearts. I know I said it up front in the introduction of this book, but it bears repeating. I am incredibly proud to be a part of this clan, and I thank them for putting up with all my craziness through the years.

Bernice and Leonard Lavin

My Mom and Dad

You need luck in raising kids, but you also need boundaries, lots of communication — and you need to BE THERE.

One Goal

My parents were hugely successful in business; they were the founders of the Alberto Culver Company. They had three children: my older brother, Scott, my younger sister, Karen, and me. They loved all of us very much. There's no question whatsoever about that. My parents had grown up in homes that were way less than affluent. My mother's mom kicked her husband out of the house for being a drinker. They never divorced, but she raised her three kids alone on her salary; she worked for General Electric. This was the 1930s and early 1940s when very few moms worked outside of the house. I remember my mother telling stories of her family going to the movies one child at a time, because there was never enough money for all the kids to go. They didn't have anything left over for "extras."

My father's dad was a salesman and, some say, a bookie on the side. My father's mom was a sweet soul. I'm not exactly sure of the whole story here, but while there was food on the table, there was not a lot of extra cash. The reason for sharing this background is, in part, to explain why my mom and dad always wanted us to have lots of things—pretty much whatever we wanted. That came with a lot of love and a lot of caring, but my parents were also working hard together

to build a company. They traveled a great deal. There wasn't a lot of discipline in our house concerning schoolwork. Who can really pinpoint all the reasons, but my gorgeous older brother had huge issues all through school (wild child) and my younger sister was always a free spirit. I have jokingly said that I was adopted; if I didn't look so much like my mom I would still wonder. The three of us were incredibly different. My brother got into serious drugs in his teens and later died of a drug overdose when he was in his forties. My sister is sweet, kind, and frankly pretty smart; she has been and always will be a free spirit, living on her land in Colorado.

Fully disclosing all of this is to help you understand why I had one goal in my life. It was to raise kind, caring, competent kids who would grow into capable adults. That was my mission, and I worked incredibly hard to make that happen. You need luck in raising kids, but you also need boundaries, lots of communication—and you need to BE THERE. I learned some things along the way. This is an attempt to share some of those "wisdoms."

But first a few thoughts from a great working mom…

Raising Kids...
and a Few Thoughts on
Being a Working Mom

"Prioritize. Focus. Build in real time for you. Learning to say, 'Sorry, I can't; I'm a little overwhelmed right now' is perfectly okay."

Let Them Be Creative

I have heard this several times now, and it makes great sense. Don't get in the way of a child's creativity. Allowing creativity to flourish can help kids find themselves in difficult times. We often want our children to color in the lines, not make a mess, clean up, and put everything away. I have heard several child psychologists over the years tell their audiences that kids need places to get dirty, stay dirty, and play without limits—whatever without limits means. The essence is to have someplace where the kids can paint, work with clay, play in the sand, or whatever; it helps unleash their sense of play and creativity.

In our home, we had an old storage room that actually had a drain in the floor. I painted the walls a light blue, and after that my kids would spend hours painting the walls with water. The paint color on the walls was great. When it was wet, it became a darker blue, so my children actually thought they were painting; and when the walls dried, the children started all over again. Water and a paint brush could keep them busy to their hearts' content. We also used this room to play at a sink with water and bubbles, mop the floor with real water, blow bubbles in the middle of the winter—and more. If you are ever lucky enough to re-do a home, think about adding a little play room with a drain. It is GREAT.

We built a great garage at our lake house and made it a little bit deeper than the length of a car. We added a couple of inexpensive kitchen cabinets and a sink for arts and crafts. In the summertime, the cars come out of the garage and we bring out a kids' table and chairs. It becomes Play-Doh city so all those nasty pieces of Play-Doh don't become part of our rugs. Don't get me wrong, we LOVE Play-Doh; just keep it where it is easy to clean up. We also have an easel and finger paints. The doors are open to the sunshine and we paint away!

> *Allowing creativity to flourish can help kids find themselves in difficult times.*

Three Envelopes

If you give an allowance, hopefully your kids will have done something to earn it. Whatever those chores may be, payment of an allowance is a good opportunity to give them three zippered pouches and to encourage that they: 1) save some, 2) give some (as in philanthropy and helping others), and 3) spend some. Starting very early on teaching that it is important to save as well as help others is a great foundation.

Toddlers Who Scream, and Adults Who Don't

I have no professional training whatsoever in wrangling toddlers, but I do have a lot of practical experience as a mother and grandmother, and this has always worked for me. When your little ones are throwing a tantrum, get down to their level. In a soft voice, tell them to scream and cry all they want and when they are done with their tantrum, to come and see you because there'll be a treat. (My thanks to my friend, Rachel, for this one.) Go and read a magazine in a place where they can clearly see you. Pay NO attention to them. The noise will eventually stop. It really does show them that you will not respond to this kind of behavior.

Another of my tricks that I learned when my children were very young and in a screaming mode or whining like crazy was to whisper. I would look at my child and not say anything for a slow count to thirty. And then I would whisper a few words, and they usually would quiet down enough to hear me. Sometimes I would even mouth the words. It wasn't so much to get them to hear me at that point but rather to get them to quiet down so they would be ready to hear me. It is so tempting to yell right back at your kids. Their behavior is totally unacceptable, but they can't hear you when they are so upset—so don't even try. You might try the silent treatment while you are looking right at their little faces and then whisper. Half the trick is to stop the screaming in the first place.

Pay no attention to them.

Maintaining the Peace

My three kids are about three-plus years apart. Our home was created to be a safe haven for all of us. I know that sounds a little "up there," but we had a few simple rules:

1. **If your friends come over and they won't let the younger kids play, send your friends home.** (Our house was pretty cool with lots of toys; no one wanted to go home.) Over time, some kids were asked to leave, and the message was sent loud and clear: the littler kids were "allowed" to stay.

2. I listen to people's issues all day at work. I don't want to be in the middle of my kids fighting with each other at home. Perhaps a little dramatic, but when my kids were older and started fighting, each trying to get my attention, I locked myself in the bathroom and told them when they stopped fighting I would come out. I had enough of that stuff at work. In other words, **don't give more attention to bad behavior**.

Not a Good Time To Visit Disney World

My daughter was a little over two and had just been potty-trained. We were so proud of her that we took her with us to Disney World. HUGE MISTAKE. Her older brothers taught her to drink from a drinking fountain. DOUBLE TROUBLE. First, we would visit every water fountain she saw, and then we would wait in line for twenty-five minutes; Lizzy would start jumping up and—of course—she had to go to the bathroom. At the time, all of Disney's bathrooms were blue or tan. I think I saw them all and made it to very few rides. I will never forget visiting the bathroom on that trip, and my sweet little girl turned to me and asked, "Are there pigs in here, Mommy?" I can just hear myself muttering under my breath as I wiped off one more toilet seat, "There must have been a pig in here!" Careful of oh-so-little ears.

When the Babies Are Teething

We have eight-month-old infants, and they are suffering with teething. Try this: make popsicles out of bottled spring water. Get simple, small-size popsicle molds and freeze nonflavored spring water. Always dip the water popsicle in clear water when removing it from the freezer to make sure it never sticks to their little lips. Of course you have to hold it, and it's a little messy, but the babies love it.

We Called It the Punishment Pen

Even writing that title makes me laugh. Only it wasn't so funny. My middle child, Peter, was, shall we say, "willful." He was the hardest of my three kids to control when he was a toddler. He was very bright and thought the world should answer to him. There would be lots of times when I would look at that beautiful child of mine and say only to myself, "I know I love you, sweet Pete, but I don't like you very much right now." After several tries of a regular time out, none of which was effective, I took a playpen and put it in another room of our house and called it the punishment pen. My child never knew I called it that, of course, but I sure did. Peter hated being in a playpen at any time, so this worked well as a time-out place until he was three and could climb out. This little monkey of mine would be very angry when he was put in his special time-out place; I put magazines in the "pen" with him, and he would rip them apart to his heart's content. After a while, I would peek around the corner and then stomp my feet so he knew I was coming back. Five minutes or so usually did the trick.

Three Hand Squeezes

Sometimes you are with your child when the verbal words "I love you" just can't be spoken. So when my children were very small we had a secret code. **Three quick hand squeezes meant I LOVE YOU.** I will tell you I used that well into their teens. They would grin and bear it as they got older, but it sure did make me feel good.

How I Love the Word "Sure"

Sure!

When my kids were little, I brainwashed them to always answer any request of mine with the word "SURE!" "Lizzy, can you come help me clean up these toys?" **"Sure, Mommy!"** I started this "brainwashing" when they were about two years old. I taught my children to answer "sure" the same way I taught them to say "please" and "thank you." I used repetition—and lots of it. But I will tell you it is a GREAT answer to any request. When they were a bit older, my kids would sometimes say "sure" in a sarcastic way, but it was still a whole lot better than their whining about something I asked them to do. Another thing I did to turn a negative into a positive was to never allow the words "I'm bored" to be used in our house. It's easy to eliminate those words when the minute they are said, you have a project or task for your kids to do. How in the world can children be bored when they have music, toys, books, games, friends, and a dog etc., etc., etc. So we never had to listen to these kids say, "I'm bored." And life was so much more pleasant.

OUT OF TOWN:
THE TREASURE HUNT

My job required that I had to be out of town for business. Thankfully, in my kids' early years, it wasn't a crazy amount of travel, but I had no choice. I had to go. We had a very good housekeeper who the kids loved, but I also tried to have my in-laws come into town and stay at our house any time I was gone for more than a day or two. Of course I wanted to call my kids before bedtime each night to tell them how much I loved them. That was usually a mistake; it too often ended with tears—until I invented the After-Dinner Treasure Hunt. When my kids would start to melt down on the phone with me, I would say, "Guys, wait, wait. I think there is a treasure hidden in our house! I need you to go and find it." Excited and laughing, they would take off to hunt down the treasure. "The first clue is in the fruit bowl on the kitchen table." And I could hang up with a smile on my face as I pictured them having fun running to find the treasures.

It's so easy. Take little squares of paper and write down a hint. I would usually have five or six clues before they could find the treasure. Obviously, the clues and the treasures were age-appropriate. I started this game when my kids were little—three or four years old—and it continued for many years. The older kids helped the younger ones, and it was always fun. I would send them from the fruit bowl, to behind the drapes in the living room, to under my bed upstairs, to the basement where we had huge blocks—and then to the treasure. The treasures when they were young could be bags of mini cookies, a special dessert each day, a bottle of bubble bath, a book, new pajamas, or small toys. I often gave them things I would have given them anyway. But presenting them as part of this game made it extra fun.

As they got older, it could be a five-dollar bill they could take to the drug store and pick their own treat. Sometimes it was their Halloween costume (that I had to buy anyway), new school supplies, or mittens. As long as the treasure came with a piece of candy, gum, or animal crackers, I was golden. Besides, **we all know the treasure hunt was for ME—a way to say goodnight to my kids and have them happy and excited instead of focused on my being away.**

BUILD IN
100-PERCENT KID TIME

As a working mom, I literally tried to build in special times with my kids when they knew I was 100 percent theirs. As an example, we had "Mommy/Lizzy outings" where Lizzy called the shots. Most of the time we would end up in a mall visiting the pet shop so she could play with the puppies. When she was older we would go "new gym shoe shopping"; it usually took us several days and fifteen shoe stores for her to find the very best ones, but it was all special time, so who cares. Of course, French fries found their way in there somewhere, or California Pizza Kitchen as she got older. I made real time for my kids every day, but I also worked hard to find big chunks of time when I was all theirs, as in "Mom will join you in whatever activities you want—playing at the playground, reading books, building a castle, painting, playing catch, etc." That is real power in a six-year-old's hands. All too often we get busy and our kids watch us do our work. There is learning in that as we are modeling behavior. But carving out chunks of time in each week to focus totally and solely on my kids made me feel better as a working mom and made them feel great.

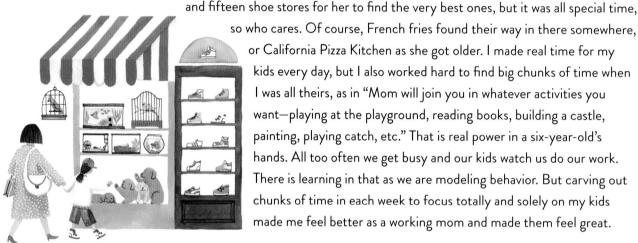

On vacations, I tried my best to have all days be "kid time." We loved playing on the beach and building giant sand castles complete with moats, bridges, flags, and even little people and animals. We were in Florida for a week after Christmas and our castles became a daily activity. I was literally in the sand with my kids for hours at a time. One day a woman came up to me and said, "I have been watching you for three days. I will double whatever you are making to come and be our nanny." That one still makes me chuckle.

Every morning I could be found in my home office from about five until seven, working. (Don't be too impressed with that. I can't stay up past nine thirty at night.) From about six a.m. on, my kids knew they had my ear, and we would hold endless conversations. Of course, I was home most nights after work, and we lived four miles from my office—so I could make it home quickly or get to a school event. But knowing that I would be in a given place every day at a given time was a good thing in our home. Of course, I traveled some but, for the most part, **my children knew where I would be and knew that I would stop whatever I was working on early in the morning and be there for them.**

HAVING KIDS WHO ARE SUCCESSFUL
WHEN THEY'RE THIRTY

My oldest son, Craig, was put in the lowest reading group in first grade. I was dumbfounded. He was smart and energetic, but I later found out that while all the other (highly competitive) moms had taught their kids to read before they started school, I had not. OMG, I couldn't believe what I had done to my son. I immediately created homemade flash cards, and we reviewed them at breakfast and dinner every day. After a month, he moved up one reading level and six weeks later, he moved up another level; he stayed in the next-to-highest level and did great. But I had a new mission: I would not think of doing anything after work until HOMEWORK WAS DONE—not my homework, his. This went on through first and second grade.

Luckily for me, I went to a YPO University in the spring of his second-grade year and heard two fantastic speakers talk about raising kids. Basically, they convinced me over the two-day seminar that what I needed to do was build resilient kids who could thrive when they were adults—even if that meant they got C's or B's instead of A's in school. The argument was pretty convincing: if you do your kids' homework, you are pretty much telling them they can't do it without you. You are setting them up to fail if they can't count on you being by their sides all the time to help them get through school and life. And frankly, it is often easier to just do the work for them. *Don't*—even if it means a lousy grade. You are hurting, not helping. That weekend changed my life and my kids' lives, and I am positive it was for the better. Sure, I quizzed them on spelling words and very occasionally helped with a major project. But 95 percent or more of their work from that point on was done exclusively by them. I am positive it helped me to raise capable adults.

If you do your kids' homework, you are pretty much telling them they can't do it without you.

Get a Toy, Give a Toy

Our children always received a lot of stuff for Christmas, birthdays, or just because. Our rule (to try to build generous, giving kids) was if you received a new toy, you then had to give an old toy to kids who didn't have many toys. It was comical. When they were little, they would get a Star Wars landing pad (huge) and give away one G.I. Joe little guy—but it still was a great concept. It also helps when they get a little older by keeping the amount of stuff in your house to a little more manageable level.

I also **found it very important to limit the number of toys my young children had at one time.** We had a "back basement" sort of storage room, and my kids will remember the stacks of games, crafts, blocks, and Playmobil sets that would be organized and waiting for them when they wanted to "trade in" one toy for another. There were, of course, baskets of toys that stayed out all the time, but there were also many items that were put away. This helped in a couple ways. First, I couldn't stand all the Playmobil pieces mixed in with the Lincoln Logs mixed in with hundreds of Lego blocks and, believe me, I personally sorted this mess too many times! So, keeping a rule that half of everything was away on the shelf helped with keeping pieces straight. And, **more importantly, I believe when children have everything within their reach, nothing is special to them.** Having less to focus on limits distractions and adds interest in and appreciation for the toys in front of them. So the "half away" concept worked well for us for years.

Still Too Many Toys

A couple of times a year the clutter would just get to me. We had our rule, "one toy in, one toy out," but that was never enough. A big toy with twenty parts would come in, and a small stuffed animal would go out. So, when my kids were not around, I would get a big black garbage bag and go and collect some toys from their rooms and the play area. I would take my "bags full"—sometimes way more than one—to the attic, where they would stay for three or four months. Sometimes I got caught and would have to go up and "find" the missing toy. I did this for years and years, moving from toys to sports equipment to clothing. But most of the time my bags found their way to Goodwill a few months later. It works!

Years later I tried the same black-bag trick with Bobby's old (ugly) sweaters and worn-out golf shirts. It didn't work quite as well—my poor housekeeper got blamed for shrinking a whole lot of stuff that I "just had to give away"—but those just had to go! Busted!

Adopt a Family at Christmas

Every Christmas we adopt several families with lots of kids and lots of need. Together, my kids and I shop, wrap, and make the holiday incredibly special for other families. When they were young, the kids also had to contribute some of their own allowance to help buy gifts. It was a special time for us to be together as all my kids worked hard to make the holiday special for our adopted families. I will say sometimes we over-bought (a lot) as they were sure more clothes and toys were needed. But to this day my grown kids adopt families.

Room Mom

As a working mom, I found it easy to be a "room mom." I could provide all the treats and take a couple of half-days off to partake in special classroom activities. It also allowed me to avoid so much of the politics I found on other PTO committees while still participating in the school in an important way. My kids loved making the party bags and holiday treats with me and, frankly, it was a fun way to be a real part of their school life.

Eliminate "Failure" and Encourage Learning

Helping your children to be resilient is probably the greatest skill you can teach. Allowing your children to "fail" will help them grow. But the whole concept of failure isn't particularly helpful. If you try, you either succeed or you learn something. Think about it. How powerful is the ability to try and try again? We finally develop a cure for a disease after decades of trial and discovery. Or that local ball team that you thought would never make the playoffs keeps trying until they break through. It's not failure if you learn something—even if what you learned is that a given approach didn't work.

Getting a D on a math test presents an opportunity to learn something: How would you go about studying differently? Who could help you? Why did you think you were ready for that test? Parents all too often want perfection. Perfection is a lousy way to live your life, and it kills resilience.

We all want our children to grow into happy, positive adults. The world our children and grandchildren will grow up in is changing exponentially faster than when we grew up. We have been told our kids will have multiple jobs over the course of their lives. It's critical to teach your children to be adaptive, resilient, resourceful, and open to learning, changing, and understanding that we all get "do-overs." You learn far more from things that didn't work out than from all those that came too easily.

When Your Kids Pull Away from Old Friends

This was a hard lesson for me, but thank goodness I learned it before I submitted more of my kids to my craziness. When my oldest was in seventh grade, he stopped seeing some of his best buddies. I kept pushing him to call two kids he had played with for years. I was friends with their moms, and these boys had practically lived in our home. Three years later, I learned why my oldest had stopped hanging around with his buddies. They were into bad stuff—in one case heavy alcohol and in the other case drugs. I still kick myself to this day. **When your children make a change in their friends, LET IT GO.** They are telling you something, and it can happen as early as fifth to eighth grade. Scary but true.

In Junior High: Assume Nothing

I think I am still surprised by how much this surprised me. Our PTO wanted to do a survey of all the parents of children in our village's junior high. I had a lot of experience with surveys, and so I offered to create the survey and have the results tallied. The questions ranged from curfew times, the amount of money to spend on a gift, and what kind of movies parents allowed their kids to see (as in ratings), to how much freedom kids were allowed to have without supervision and whether the parents would let their child go to an unsupervised party, go downtown alone, or walk to a party at night a couple of miles away. Was an overnight with boys and girls acceptable if done in a school setting? What was the amount given for allowance? And it included many more questions.

My surprise came in how far off I was from the results of the majority. I guess I had assumed all our villagers thought the same. But it seemed we had a much tighter leash on our kids than so many others did and for me, movies at that age were still for entertainment, not violence or sex. Curfew and walking alone at night were other areas where I was in a different place than my peers. This survey opened my eyes and had me directly asking the parents of my children's friends a whole lot more questions—nicely, of course. And I aligned with people who thought more like I did. The lesson here, of course, is don't assume you know what others are thinking or what their values are.

And I aligned with people who thought more more like I did.

Use the Bad Example

I have mentioned my brother, Scott, died of a drug overdose. It was awful to lose him so young. But even more horrible, when he was alive, was to wait and watch my family over the holidays expecting my brother to show up at any time and then be disappointed. My nephew flew from Australia to be with his dad every Christmas. Half the time, Scott wouldn't show, and three days after Christmas, he might show up completely out of it.

So instead of hiding my brother's problem, I used it

My kids saw that behavior over the years and were with their uncle when he was clearly not in his right mind. I used the "Uncle Scott" example all the time. I showed my kids what happened when they did drugs of any kind, and I promised them, at least a hundred times, that if I ever caught them using drugs they would be sent away from all their friends to a school in Scotland. I meant it. God knows I prayed a lot because we all live in a world where drug use is just too incredibly prevalent in our communities and even in our schools. And of course, we spent a great deal of time talking about all the horrors of addiction and the unintended consequences of trying drugs even just one time. So instead of hiding my brother's problem, I used it—and to my knowledge, my kids never did drugs. Unfortunately, we did have a few alcohol incidents but never hard drugs. Gosh, it's tough raising teenagers.

WHEN THINGS
GET TOUGH

When my son Peter was growing up he had a wonderful friend named Billy Nickels. We have a couple of important "wisdoms" that came from knowing and loving Billy. When Billy was two years old, he contracted a virus that caused him, as a toddler, to need an immediate kidney transplant. Peter and Billy became best buddies when they were very young and stayed that way throughout Billy's life.

Billy was precious; he was smart and kind and an athlete, which made sense as his parents were all these as well. I remember being in a "moms and munchkins" class at the community center and getting a note in the mail that said something like, "In class there is a child, whose parents wish to remain anonymous, who has kidney disease and many childhood illnesses that could present serious consequences. The family wishes to keep their identity private so their child is treated totally as an equal, but please inform us if any of your children come down with chicken pox or similar illnesses." So, for the first several years of Peter and Billy's friendship, we did not have a clue. From the ages of three to six or seven, all kids grow at different times—one child is short and another is tall. It makes no difference. But over the years as the boys grew older, it was clear that the meds would prevent Billy from growing normally, and the height difference became something quite real.

Billy was a regular guest at our meals and was at our home often, as Peter was at Billy's. These kids were pretty much inseparable. Jump ahead to sixth, seventh, and eighth grade. My son Craig had to wear a Milwaukee brace (see "Finding Your Strength" in the "Tough Times" chapter). So, the games our kids played with their friends were creative and sometimes comical. Basketball games often took place in our basement, and more often than not, the kids played it on their knees. Not my invention at all, just a leveling of the playing field for these incredible kids. The boys may have "seen" Craig's awful brace and Billy's height issues, but it simply didn't matter. They saw past these "disabilities" and came up with games and activities that allowed all of them to participate and be competitive. They created their own fantasy football league, played way too much poker, cards, Gameboy, Nintendo, soft bat baseball, nerf football—whatever they could do within Craig's restrictions and Billy's disadvantaged height and medical issues. These boys made life happen—it was extraordinary. I closed my eyes to the "gambling." Whatever worked to make these young lives normal was okay with me. I could not have been more proud. There were times when Billy was at our house for four hours and then had to go home for a couple of hours to rest and, in later years, sometimes have dialysis. "Okay. Come back for dinner. We're making burgers."

Over the years, Billy needed to be hospitalized a number of times. Many of the kids in his class were attentive and visited when Billy was in the hospital, but many weren't around when he was home and doing fine. Peter was the opposite. He never wanted to visit Billy in the hospital, and he was always there when he was well. I talked to Billy's mom about this, and she agreed that was the way to play it. Billy hated being in the hospital and didn't like people to see him sick. With Peter, his relationship was always "normal," and that was the way they wanted to keep it. We took the family's lead and let the boys

My opinion is if you love your kids, they will be okay. LOVE is pretty magical stuff.

Let the guilt go.

Some moms work because they must, some moms work because they want to, and some work because they need to and they want to. I hope you are one of those moms who likes your job regardless of why you work. It helps a whole lot if you love what you are doing because being a happy mom is a good thing to show your kids. If you are unhappy, think about how you can make a change.

It is amazing how everyone who has a child is an expert on raising kids and is sure they know what is best. Also, it is crazy how opinionated other people are about your life. Try hard to let that go also.

My opinion is if you love your kids, they will be okay. LOVE is pretty magical stuff. Yes, your child would rather you stay home and play with them every day of your life. That does not make them a better child. Going to work and coming home shows them that they can count on you and do well on their own. That too is a good thing to learn. Hopefully you have a good child-care option. If you don't, work hard to make a better choice. That is really important. I can't imagine being at work if I didn't feel good about who was caring for my children. Private help, child-care centers, grandparents, or friends all can be great partners in helping us grow our kids.

One of my very best friends lives in the south, is incredibly smart, but did not work after she had kids. Over the years, we were together most years traveling somewhere with our children, and she would comment every so often about how "normal and nice" my kids were. People: moms who work have nice, normal kids too. I don't brag about much, but my kids are grown, and I sure do like them—and they like me. They have jobs, they have families they love, and they consider themselves to be very lucky. They are smart, humble, and kind—even though I was a working mom.

Going to work and coming home shows them that they can count on you and do well on their own.

A MOM'S
LEGACY

One of the great satisfactions I get from public speaking is the chance to salute, promote, and encourage working moms. Still today, when you would think most of the battles had been won, there continue to be raging debates about leaning in, equal pay, promotion tracks, and work–life balance. So much of this obscures the tremendous contributions that moms make, both working moms and those who stay at home. My respect for both groups is unbounded.

It's not easy being a mom. I can't think of a more important job or one that can have a bigger impact on tomorrow's world.

I have the privilege of speaking to numerous groups every year. When it's appropriate and the talk is to women, I often close with the following:

Being a working mom means you have to miss a lot. We can never be at every concert, game, or field trip—but perhaps we leave a greater legacy.

A working mom teaches her daughter every day that being feminine is a good thing, but so is strength, independence, and self-worth.

We raise our sons with the understanding that women are to be treated as equals, that a mom can be a great cook, a great business person, and a respected partner in life and in work.

Working moms make America's workplaces and communities better for all of us. I believe the work environment is a little kinder and a little more values-based, as we carry our family values into the workplace. The smart companies realize how these values build a better workforce for tomorrow while they give a powerful boost to the sales and profits of industry today. The path we forge will, we hope, make it easier for our daughters and granddaughters and build a place where our sons can be better men.

Building Family Traditions

I have many family traditions I started with my kids, and I'm hoping some will last the test of time for generations to come. Life just goes too fast, and these are still special memories.

Making Wishes

We take walks and make a "wish" on a gate, a tree, or some object that signifies the end of our walk. Silly, but all my kids know I do this and they will do it too. **How can another wish or two hurt?**

Family Time

When kids are young introduce the words **"Family Time."** Make that mean it's a time we sit down (or do something) as a family, with only our family. Take walks, read a book, play a game, watch a movie, sing around a piano, go to church, take a special trip, or cook a family dinner. By building these words into their vocabulary, it also **builds the special concept of family as a unit when the kids are very young**. Keep this concept going throughout your lives. Don't overuse it, or use it as an excuse to keep your older kids from doing something fun with others; always allow it to be powerful and special.

We would spend every Christmas with my parents at our farm in Florida. For a solid week we never left our farm; we just stayed there doing fun things with each other. Then we would drive to spend time with my in-laws. These vacations were "double perfect" in my mind. Time spent with your children when they are little is so crucial, but it's even more important when they are teenagers. We swam, read, played tennis, looked at the new baby foals, ate all meals together, watched movies, played games; we were just a family without all the "outside" interruptions. And it was pretty special to vacation every year with each set of grandparents. Also incredibly special were the trips my kids took with my parents, where they learned to fish, play poker, love horse racing, value nature, and enjoy almost any sporting event. Most of all, they saw in action the amount of work that followed my family everywhere. Work hard, play hard—but

Family Time

THE BIG LESSON:
No matter what you choose to do,
do it together.

understand that people are counting on you and you need to be connected even on vacation. Once again, living our core value of working hard.

Vegetable Garden

Plant a vegetable garden with your kids. Tomatoes and peppers grow pretty easily if planted in a place with lots of sunlight—whether in pots on a balcony or a little plot in your garden. I did this with my kids and it warmed my heart to see my daughter doing it with her daughters as well.

Tribute at Birthdays

As the kids get older, introduce a speech about your child at his or her birthday dinner. Focus on all the fun stuff you love about them and the funny memories from the last year. Have the other kids contribute. Take a little time and make it important. It will be a memory that lasts a lifetime. My father has given a Thanksgiving toast for every year of our lives. It's always something special.

Good Will

When my kids were a little older, at least once a year we would clean out their rooms and closets. They would spend a couple of hours with me choosing what they would give away; the goal was to donate 20 percent of their stuff. It helped to teach them that other people need clothes, toys, and sports equipment. They learned from early ages to share, and as they got older, they would come to me when they heard someone's house had burned down or a family needed help because the parents had lost their jobs. It was a great way to help build compassionate kids.

Pitching In

At Christmas, we would hold an all-company event for the children of all our employees at an indoor amusement park. We gave away gifts at various carnival stations and, of course, Santa would come. It was heartwarming to see our whole workforce with their kids. My children were guests until they were twelve and then every year they were recruited to work. It was great to see them helping all the little ones and being a part of our "family business." They did this for years. I am convinced that all this exposure to our workforce was a great factor in building their own work ethic.

A Few More Ideas

Here are some additional ideas for mom, dad, or grandparents to consider to build traditions through the years:

- From my friend Marty Whealy: give ten cards for a tenth birthday.
- Pick up a shell each time you go to the beach with your kids and display them in a glass bowl.
- A week before Christmas, buy seven books for your children. Unwrap one each night as you count down to Christmas.
- If you own a house, plant a tree on your property for each birth.
- Do something special for a twenty-first birthday.
- Pick apples every fall. Go to pumpkin farms at Halloween. Visit the best windows in town at Christmas and spend the night in the city. We would repeat certain things every year, and we created wonderful traditions with our kids.
- Hang bird feeders in your garden and see nature come alive.
- Take walks in every season. My children used to make fun of me always exclaiming about the autumn colors. Not anymore. They too love sunsets, the leaves changing, snow falling, and flowers blooming. Share your passions. This love of nature became part of their core.
- Take a weekend away with your child and their friends. I am positive I got to know my children so much better when I spent chunks of time with their friends.

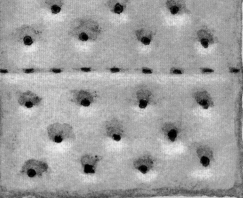

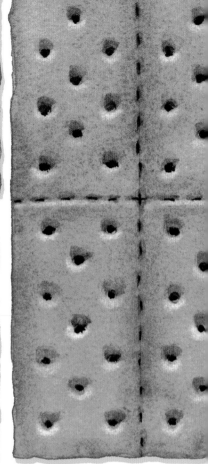
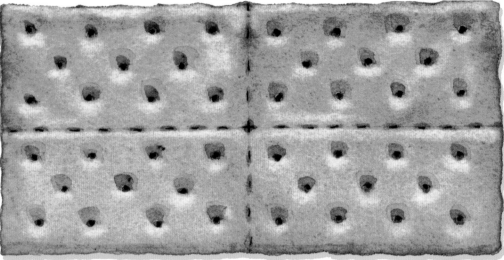
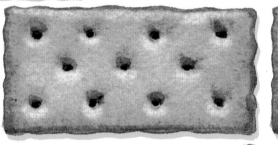
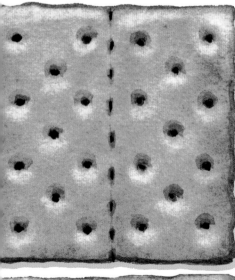

Building the Grandma Brand

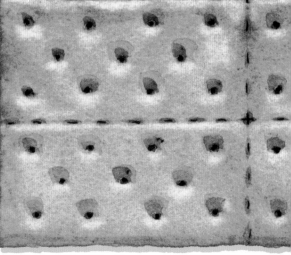
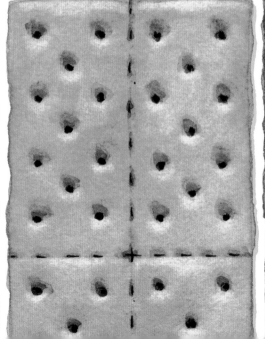

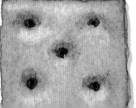

More Traditions

Yes, of course, you are a terrific grandma. At this very moment, I have six grandkids three and under and Bobby's daughter, Kate, and her husband, Dan, have two little boys, almost four and two. And I am FUN. My grandkids call me CC. But right now, every time Alex and Scotty see me their eyes light up, and they hold up their little arms and scream "GOLF CART!" We ride in the golf cart for at least thirty minutes every morning they are at the lake. Lake Geneva has been shortened to Ninja by their little minds. I guess that sounds close (Ninja? Geneva?). We visit the park (a mini playground) and the lake; we get graham crackers (BIG cookies!) and go bumpety bump on the uneven bricks as we make our way to see the leaves, boats, ducks, and diggers (Alex is into trucks and cars, and there is always a digger somewhere near where we live at the lake). We put our feet in the water, go puddle jumping, and throw stones. It is the hit of their day at Lake Geneva and incredibly fun for me too; we probably did these activities at least twenty times last summer.

I believe building traditions is important and fun. Ask a young adult what traditions they remember, and you will be surprised how important some of their memories truly are. So, I am one who will drive myself crazy leaving "things" in my will to my kids and grandkids. I will go to the trouble of picking specific things that I want them to have. These are things that I hope one day will mean something to them and help build the continuity of family that is so important to me.

In my mind, that sort of connects with my wanting them to **have special experiences JUST WITH ME** that mean something to them over time. So, some things to think about: What are ways to build the "Grandma Brand?" That may sound commercial to you, but I have a lot of expertise in marketing and branding, and I know that big brands stand for something and repeat their message again and again. Of course, my main message is that I love them, will always be there for them, and want to help instill all the values we as a family believe in. But I also think about traditions that can mean a lot. So, while I was thinking of concepts for me, I thought I would share the following:

Think of building a tradition as simple as the golf cart ride (as long as they will go with me) at Lake Geneva. One day this will transition to a car, with me at the wheel—and then one day likely they will be driving me! Another tradition can start with an annual gift or you can build up to a trip, a car, or something incredible. Over the months or years, the collection, the event, or the experience develops into something wonderful. You can start this when they are infants, when they are ten, or whenever you are moved to do so. Any and all can be pretty darn exciting.

I love to give gifts, and the "immediate joy" is fun to see on a child's face. But when you think of your own memories, you most likely remember places you went and things you did together with a grandparent. And even more fun is the building of experiences that repeat. Here are some gifts, collections, and experiences to think about:

You most likely remember places you went and things you did together with a grandparent.

Experiences

- Forget the "stuff" and be the "experience" guide. Take your grandchildren to museums, an airshow, a musical, or on an overnight campout. The concept, of course, is to "package" the experience and call it the same thing time after time. Send an invitation that looks the same each time to "announce the adventure" in a similar way. Adventures with CC (I really like this one)!

- Build Legos together month after month, culminating in a trip to the Lego store.

- Invite the kids for an overnight and have something special for breakfast: pancakes in any shape they like are so easy. Include fruit, nuts, and whipped cream. Or make Sunday "donut day" and share donuts with your grandkids.

- Surprise the grandchildren with tickets to a special concert or play: add culture to their lives, or be the super-cool grandma who sends her kids tickets to rock concerts, sporting events, or both—and goes with them. The idea here is to count on something that repeats over time. It's another form of "Adventures with Grandma."

- Invite all the kids to come and spend a week (or weekend) with you, and fill the time with activities from morning to night. Of course, when I invite my grandkids to Camp CC, I will find three or four events/activities that repeat each year. That's the magic of traditions.

- Hold a neighborhood parade every Fourth of July. Decorate bikes and cars and have a blast.

- Paint your granddaughter's toenails whenever she comes for a visit.

Gifts

- Purchase new gym shoes every year. Either send them to your grandchildren, or make it your thing to take them shopping.
- Buy your grandchildren a new lunch box or backpack each year.
- Buy a new first-day-of-school outfit each year. Again, take them shopping or have them send you links to items they would like from the Internet.
- Give each grandchild one fantastic ornament each Christmas. After twenty years, the children will be able to decorate a tree with sentimental memories.
- Start a collection of mini teapots or salt and pepper shakers.
- Give a leather-bound book each year, starting with fairy tales and graduating to classics.
- Assemble a Christmas village by giving one new piece every year.
- Grandma can pay for camp, gymnastics, or other experiences. But make it even more special by also giving a special flashlight, a leotard, or other tie-in. Talk with the kids or with their parents to find out what one special thing the kids want to do that you can make happen for them each year.
- Buy a quality metal car each year that can lead to a great car collection—and add to that the promise of a trip to the auto show each year.
- Give money each year to be banked until the kids are twenty-one.

Build a Snowman

So many ideas to create memories... choose a couple and build traditions!

Tea Party!

Treats to Eat!

Sleepover at Grandma's

Golf Cart!

Ho ho ho!

Donut Day!

Treats to Eat!

Horsey rides

Make music together

Easter Hunt (for a one year old)

Play dress up with your dog!

Treats to Eat!

Trips

- Take the family on a special trip once a year courtesy of Grandma. Every Christmas, your Christmas gift to your grandkids is something that relates to that trip. Assume the vacation is in February each year. The gift to the grandkids could be ski parkas or swimsuits, all wrapped up in a box with a description of the vacation location. Keeping it simple and going to a water park near a local Holiday Inn can be as fun as a trip to Colorado. It doesn't have to be crazy costly. Maybe some years you splurge more than others. You can visit the national parks or Williamsburg, rent an RV and do a road trip, or go to the big city (for us, Chicago) and spend a night or two. Imagine how incredibly fun that is year after year—a Christmas gift that lasts for months, and memories that last forever.

- Think about a trip to Disney World. You could announce a trip that will take place at the "end of this year" and send a teaser every month to the family: a Disney guidebook, a Disney toy, a Disney backpack, a Disney T-shirt. You will be a hero and the excitement can last all year long. And buy little Disney toy animals before you go, keep them in your suitcase, and put one on their pillow each night! It's cheaper and a fun treat!

- Find special travel books or mementos from special places and give a child one each year until they are twelve. On their twelfth birthday, you take them on the "special trip with Grandma and Grandpa." You have lots of years to plan a trip while exploring travel books and the Internet.

I'm choosing which couple of these I will do. My grandkids are a little small right now, but I am thinking! And of course, this concept works for a favorite niece, nephew, godchild, or anyone with whom you want to share precious memories.

Let's Go Skiing

Take me to Disney

Adventures with CC!

Sought-after treasures every time your little ones come to visit.

Keep a little zippered pouch in your purse.

Skills to Pass Along

Many of us carry memories of our grandparents and recall experiences watching them engaged in activities that they were passionate about—and sometimes allowing us to be included. These were teaching moments, and I will be sure I teach my grandkids some of the things I love to do. Whether you love to bake pies, cookies, or cupcakes; play golf, tennis, gin rummy, or Scrabble; or hike, bike, or garden, be sure to include the little ones in your life. Chances are, they might like these same things too, and they will always remember who taught them. These are memories to cherish.

Traveling with Your Adult Kids

I love to travel with my adult children and their families. And I try hard to make it as easy for them as I can by providing all the baby needs related to food, diapers, toys, equipment, etc. So, it is pretty easy to travel when I set it up. And I am very lucky: they come.

But I make it FUN for my adult kids also. When they come on a trip with me, I make dinner plans for most nights. I make it very clear that I would like to dine with them a couple of nights but they are totally free to do whatever they want otherwise. So, I have the reservations if they choose to join me, and a day or two before the evening they "call it." They take advantage of their freedom and have a date night or two, or occasionally they will meet up with friends. We have access to a beach or the pool; sometimes we are all together, and often the various families take off on their own. It makes it easy on them—and makes it fun and far less hassle than the "let's do everything together all the time" routine. We have had many fun occasions when everybody came, and I am sure it is because nothing is a "must."

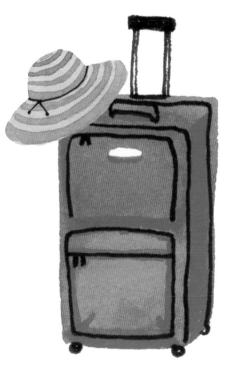

Older Parents

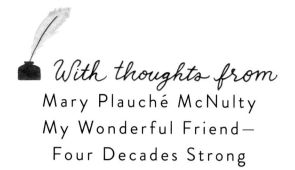

With thoughts from
Mary Plauché McNulty
My Wonderful Friend—
Four Decades Strong

On a hot August day in 1970, I followed my parents' advice and knocked on the door next to mine in my freshman dorm at Tulane. "Hi, I'm Mary," was all I could manage. Lucky for me, my next-door neighbor was Carol Lavin. She invited me not just into her room, but into her life. Thus began our forty-seven-year friendship. How was it that we bonded? I am from a small town in Louisiana, and Carol is from a Chicago business family. Despite our differences in background and geography, the raising of our three children and mothering them has been a foremost vocation for both of us. We shared new-baby worries, teenage traumas (that drove us crazy), and more recently, the season of navigating the issues of our own aging parents.

Carol and I both have fathers born in October 1919 and mothers who both our fathers would say were the prettiest girls they ever laid eyes on. Our fathers were both Navy men—World War II heroes, actually. We were unabashed "Daddy's girls." Our mothers were also our role models. We followed in their footsteps in our own lives.

I lost both my parents—my mother eighteen years ago and my father eleven years ago. Carol is blessed to still have her extraordinary father with her. She and I have shared so many moments, experiences, and insights as we have cared for our parents through their later years. Because I lost mine earlier, I felt compelled to share with her what I learned. And some of what I learned in caring for and losing my parents is this:

Sometimes, it was so frustrating, so maddening, or so sad. I felt guilty about my impatience and intolerance. In different ways, my image and definition of them was shaken—and this shook my own definition of myself. No matter how loving and comfortable my parental relationship was, there was a primal shift when they were at the end of their lives. It challenged me to be the best I could be in often adverse circumstances. I learned to always advocate for them, find patience where there was none, and always, always retain my sense of humor!

But...despite these feelings, I discovered stunning and sometimes mystical moments that are the gifts to us who are in the trenches. If we truly pay attention and come from a place of acceptance of the process, we can be peaceful and grateful even in the roughest patches. The "paying attention" part is key, not always driving the action, forcing an agenda, or controlling the outcome. Instead, listening and watching with ears and eyes filled with respect and love. Realizing that we, too, will be in their shoes someday—thus learning from them.

I always ended our conversations with, "Now, is there anything else I can do for you?" reinforcing that I was there for them, but not telling them what they needed, what to do, or how to feel.

I miss my parents. Apologies to everyone reading this, but I really did have the best parents in the world. Caring for them at the end of their lives was my privilege. And it is no surprise that my friend Carol feels the same way. She has navigated this chapter in life with grace, wisdom, and creativity—the qualities she applies to all facets of her life. I knew when I met her that day in college, and I've been reminded so many times in the last four decades, that we are so similar in what really matters. Embracing the challenge of aging parents has been just the latest chapter in our abiding friendship.

It's Never Too Late to Do Something Fabulous

As I write this, my dad is ninety-seven years old. He has always been a huge influence in my life, and I am incredibly close to him. As he says all too often, "Getting old is not for sissies." Up until about eight years ago, he walked everywhere. Now, because of spinal stenosis, he is wheelchair-bound and needs help even to move. But his faculties are all there. He reads at least one book a week and will voice his opinions about anything from politics to what I might be wearing. My dad lives in his own home with help; these are good people and someone from my family sees him very often—multiple times a week if not more.

But I am sure that "new adventures" have kept my dad alive and looking forward. We have been lucky enough to welcome new babies into this world six times in the last three years. THAT has been huge, of course. He has been excited for each one. We have also planned events that he looks forward to. We make crazy birthday plans months out. We find a way to take him to restaurants he used to love twenty-five years ago—we just go very early. We find that creating something "new" to look forward to is very important to keep him engaged.

My dad and my mom lived in the same home for decades. It was a hassle to get there, especially with the great-grandbabies. It was close to an hour away in the car, and when we would arrive for a visit dragging the babies, my dad would often need to take a nap and wanted us to wait to visit until he took a rest. Now we were up to a multiple-hour visit, and that was just hard.

My dad expressed a couple of times that maybe he should move a little closer to us. I didn't think he really meant it, but it got me thinking. I looked for a home in the town where two of my children lived and found one for sale that actually backed up to my son's house and was a block from my daughter's. I decided that I would just take a shot and buy it. I bought it in my name—and decorated it with nice furniture but not using all the great stuff from my parents' house as I didn't want to tear his home apart if my experiment didn't work out. I called it our summer cottage and, frankly, I hoped my dad would want to stay there for a couple of months at least in the summer and make it easier on all of us. I thought there was a chance if he loved it we would sell the family home. While I didn't take furniture, I went through my parents' home and took out twelve boxes of loot to make the "summer cottage" look like home.

My dad lives in California most of the time, and he came back to Chicago for a couple of months a year ago last May. Usually we would wait a couple of days for him to acclimatize to the time change, but he was anxious to see the "summer cottage" and we took him to see it the day after he returned from California. He took one look around and said to his housekeeper, "Go get my stuff"—and he has not left. Our family house of fifty years was big, but not practical for a person in a wheelchair. My dad was limited to two or three rooms at most. The new summer cottage (frankly, a lovely brick home) had a first-floor bedroom, a screened-in porch off the master bedroom, and a bathroom that had been converted and was fully handicap accessible and easy to use. The summer cottage has multiple rooms for him to enjoy. He can eat outside, in the kitchen, or in the dining room and the house, while half the size of his original, is much more conducive to company.

It was about a third of the price of his home on the lake but so much more comfortable for everyone. We sold the family home and now we are trying to fit some of the more precious furniture into the new house.

I should have made this move for him long ago. I would urge you to think about what is best for your older relatives and for the family. I promised my dad I would never put him in a nursing home, but I didn't promise I wouldn't move him. We found the most important thing was to have people around my dad as often as possible. He has twenty-minute visits several times a day from his great-grandkids with one of their parents. And at other times, his grandkids (my adult children) pop in for coffee. IT IS SO NICE. And everything is new and fresh. I am convinced that the newness and the understanding that there is "new stuff" to look forward to even at ninety-seven is a real motivation for my dad.

An Idea from My Friend Marty

Marty bought a precious little tree for her parents. She e-mailed all their family members with kids asking them to please make small ornaments out of construction paper and write sentiments (and memories) on them for their grandma and grandpa (and, for some, their great-grandma and -grandpa). The response from their family was incredibly moving. They all mailed the paper ornaments to one family member, who hung them on the little tree and presented it to Grandma and Grandpa. It was a deeply meaningful and priceless gift.

25 GIFTS
UNDER GRANDMA'S TREE

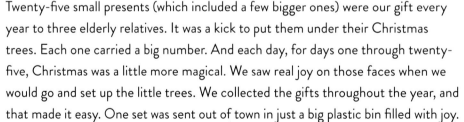

Twenty-five small presents (which included a few bigger ones) were our gift every year to three elderly relatives. It was a kick to put them under their Christmas trees. Each one carried a big number. And each day, for days one through twenty-five, Christmas was a little more magical. We saw real joy on those faces when we would go and set up the little trees. We collected the gifts throughout the year, and that made it easy. One set was sent out of town in just a big plastic bin filled with joy.

Camp Packages for Eighty-Year-Olds

I was walking through a retirement home with Bobby's mom. We always took her something like a plant, a cake, or some fun gift. I finally realized she was parading us through the whole place so her "camp mates" at the retirement home could see that we loved her enough to visit and bring her treats. So, for a kick, I went and bought twenty items, scribbled off twenty cute notes—so easy to do on a computer with clip art. I made twenty of the same labels and mailed these to her once a week until they were gone. We decorated each outer package with stickers. She loved it. I can still see her walking through her retirement home with these packages, showing all her friends and saying, "Look what someone who loves me sent today!"

Look what someone who loves me sent today!

TRANSITIONS TO
ASSISTED LIVING

When my friend Christa, who works with me and is helping me to edit this book, read my stories on older parents, she suggested I include a lesson she learned. It concerns her parents, but the whole "not letting people into retirement communities" was new news to me—so I asked her to share her story:

Most of us hope we're not a burden to our kids in our older age. But as people age, some lose sight of what may or may not be in their best interest long term.

My parents love their home, social club, and familiarity with shopping in their town. But as they were nearing eighty, they began slowing down—Mom physically and Dad cognitively. The responsibilities of maintaining their home, cooking, managing their finances, planning vacations, and all the rest were more challenging. We (their three children) took the lead in suggesting and researching senior living communities for them. We shared the "pros" of making that transition: the opportunity to make new friends while they were still healthy; having meals, activities, and medical personnel available on site; having access to transportation; and more. But my parents had no interest in moving to an "old people's home," losing their independence, and leaving the home they loved.

When that first approach didn't work, we got "real" with my mom, reminding her that my dad's early-stage dementia would likely progress, limiting his ability in the future to pass the cognitive medical exam most senior living communities require for admission. We learned that many communities offer "care until the day you die" for a cost that increases as the care increases. However, these communities are businesses, and they manage their financial risk by only admitting people who are pretty darn healthy. People who are already presenting signs of illness are left to choose from nursing homes or specialty care facilities, such as a memory care unit for those with late-stage dementia or Alzheimer's. Sadly, my mom and dad concluded they would be able to take care of each other, no matter what might happen.

One year later, my dad's dementia progressed. At my mom's request, we reconnected with several of the communities only to learn that my dad would no longer be able to pass the medical exam. Their options now are to remain together in their home (and hire in-home help) or have my dad moved to a nursing home or memory care facility. For now, they are remaining in their home, and my mom is now my dad's primary caregiver—which is overwhelming and leaves her in tears many days. It wasn't my parents' desire to be in this situation; they just always felt it was too early to make a move.

My husband and I have decided not to make the same mistake. We're going to start thinking about our plans for our eighties when we are in our sixties and fine-tune them in our early seventies. I suggest you put that on your to-do list too!

And a Couple More Things

- *If one of your parents refuses to give up their car keys when you know they shouldn't be driving, don't hesitate to call their doctor to share your concerns. Even if your parent has not signed a HIPAA waiver for the doctor to speak with you, the doctor can "hear you" express your concerns and take matters into his or her own hands. Thankfully, my dad is no longer driving because the state revoked his license (thanks to his doctor).*

- *Be sure to know where your parents' estate documents are located (will, revocable living trust, power of attorney for property and for health care, living will). Suggest that your parents add you or another trusted adult child as an authorized signer on their checking account or at least provide you with online access to view and monitor their spending. This might be important if your parents are unable to pay their bills for medical or other reasons, and it also allows a second set of eyes to watch for any type of scam. And offer to serve as their co-trustee if they have a revocable trust, again to provide a second pair of eyes on any legal arrangements. Being a co-trustee with your parent keeps the communication open.*

- *And finally, be careful of elder abuse; it comes in many forms. People can ask for money, items, loans, or investments—and can abuse an older person's trust. When you discover that a parent has made a decision they never would have made a decade ago, be extra cautious.*

Losing Your Filters

You have probably heard people say this and I KNOW it to be true: when people get older they lose their filters. The language can become much more colorful (to put it nicely); they have zero patience for just about anything; and more often than not, "it's all about them." Whatever traits a person displayed in their younger years become more pronounced. My dad was aggressive in life and business. He was also kind and very generous, but he had determination, strength, and an incredible work ethic. His favorite saying is, "Winners make it happen." When he was younger, that meant he could knock down solid brick walls, one way or another, whenever they stood in his way. And now that he is in his late nineties, that aggressive attitude sometimes gets him into trouble— verbally and physically. So why am I sharing this? All too many times I find myself "explaining" a behavior to someone who never knew my dad earlier in his life. My friend Mary told me a story about her mom and a doctor who called Mary a saint for putting up with her mom's attitude and behavior. Mary looked at that doctor and told him he had NO idea of the kind and caring person her mom had been for 95 percent of her life. So sometimes when I am introducing my dad to a new doctor or caregiver, I take a few minutes to explain just how extraordinary this man is—and was for the majority of his life. **Exposing people to a little of your loved one's background helps put a little dignity back in the equation.** So stand up for those you love. Show pictures, tell stories.

Pain Meds and Older Folks

Another "wisdom" I gathered was also from an episode with my dad while he was at his home in California. My father has some pain; it's not a great deal, but occasionally his legs or back give him some trouble, and he complains about it. Tylenol just didn't cut it. So after much discussion, his doctors gave him a prescription for Norco to be used occasionally if needed. He later ended up in the hospital with a UTI (urinary tract infection) and four days later, after it finally cleared, they let him go home. He has nursing care at home, and one of his nurses decided to give him Norco. Frankly, the doctor had said to lay off it due to the confusion that comes with a UTI. But the nurse thought she knew better—and this was happening over Thanksgiving. My family had flown to California to be with Dad and when we got there, the home nurses were alarmed and were telling us it was time to fly him

Heavy pain meds on top of a UTI can cause pretty big problems.

home to Chicago—that he didn't have long to live. Now, I had talked to the docs in the hospital the day prior, and I had heard nothing of the kind. So after listening to all this noise, my son and I told the nurses to stop giving him any kind of pain meds at all. We were not flying him home; we would see him in the morning. Lo and behold, I received a call at six a.m. the next day from his nurse exclaiming, "It's a miracle! He is up and talking and wants eggs." Of course, it wasn't a miracle at all, folks. Heavy pain meds on top of a UTI can cause pretty big problems. No more Norco for my dad. (I'm saying "never," but who knows?)

MAKE IT HAPPEN

M y mom had COPD (Chronic Obstructive Pulmonary Disease), and she lived with it for more than a decade. COPD makes it very hard for one to breathe. Yes, my mom smoked forever, and this disease was really hard for her and impossible for us to watch as she struggled. But my mom always was a fighter, and she remained so during all the years of her illness. And my dad dragged her everywhere, even when it wasn't such a good idea.

My parents had a very close and loving relationship, and my dad would not give up or let go in any way. My parents had lifelong friends who had this amazing boat, and they went with them to the Bahamas. For three years, my mom had refused to even consider a wheelchair, but their host was a big guy who was super important in the worlds of sports and business, and he was not having anything to do with my mom's craziness. When they arrived in the Bahamas, he asked the captain to "go get Bernice's chariot" and out came a "decked-out" wheelchair. He said to my mom, "Get in, Bernice. We are not leaving you behind." She had no choice and he "made it happen."

From then on, my mom could go places with us and accepted her limitations with grace. Sometimes you just must make it happen and, if the truth be known, I think my dad put his friend up to it. So, whatever it takes, do what is right with older folks. Sometimes you just have to take control.

Things to Think About

It's not easy getting old. For many, it becomes increasingly more difficult to do the common activities that once came so naturally. Some limitations are physical, while others are cognitive. Nevertheless, there are ways to help older folks ease into and cope better with these challenges. Here are some tips to give joy and get joy—and to help preserve their dignity.

- Bring over big-print books, big-print playing cards, and, if needed, a magnifying clip-on screen for a computer. Don't make a big deal about it: no one wants to be reminded they are losing their eyesight or other faculties. And add more lamps. Extra light is a big plus. A gift my dad loved was a mini LED flashlight. We gave him a box full to take to restaurants and elsewhere.

- Laminate a mini list of the latest meds and make sure YOU keep it in your wallet as well as in your parents' wallets; and keep it updated. Do the same with a list of all their doctors. You may need them in the middle of the night. Keep the list updated with cell phone numbers and keep it close by.

- Clothes need to be replaced more often than usual. Staining just happens more with older folks. Surprise your parents with a few new shirts or blouses on a regular basis.

- Older folks look a whole lot younger when dressed well. A hospital gown is not a good look for anyone. Try to find clothing that is easy to take off and put on, but always keep it sharp. For example, Lululemon has great black elastic-waist pants for men. Hats also do amazingly good things for older folks.

- Keep on top of grooming: hair care provides a real boost, and skin and nails—especially toenails—need regular professional attention. You can find someone who will make house calls for a manicure, pedicure, or haircut. Tell your dad that it's a therapeutic foot massage. Pay for an extra twenty minutes of foot massaging: older people don't get enough "touching."

- Get your older relatives to write (or dictate) their thoughts to your children on financial tips, i.e., how to live a solvent life.

- And there is so much more to learn: ask about their military service, business success and valued lessons, what TV and radio used to be like, and of course the story of how they met their spouse. It not only gets your parent engaged, but it shares a lot of pretty darn precious memories.

- Serve foods that are simple to cut or just precut what is served. Many older folks have trouble swallowing. Sometimes you have to thicken liquids to keep them from choking; thickeners can be found at any drug store.

- Make a family tree together. There are many names and relationships you just don't know. Take the time before it's no longer an option.

- Hearing aids: just force it!

- Hold a luncheon for your parent's four best friends. Make it special with their favorite treats. Boredom and loneliness are the enemies.

- Most older folks can't travel well alone or even with their spouse—but they love to go. Go with them; they likely will even pay for it if they have the means. This is their trip, not yours, so plan the trip around them.

- If you live where it snows, walks can be treacherous. Make sure someone is salting the footpaths. If an elderly person breaks a hip, the consequences are simply awful.

- Music is an amazing gift. We gave my dad a portable iPod player and loaded it with several hundred songs from the 1940s through the '80s, and he loves it. Music is playing all the time. Amazon Echo is fabulous too—just ask "Alexa" to play your favorite song or music genre.

- Old movies are great. For my dad, war movies always trump all else; he even enjoys the black-and-white government documentaries. My guess is he feels like he is in his early twenties as he remembers these times, hard as they were.

- Shutterfly books are so easy to make; I mix old photos with new ones. My dad looks at the couple of books I have made almost every day.

- Take the little ones around to visit often. Borrow little ones if need be!

- Older men (my dad anyway) do so much better when the physical therapist is a cute young woman, and I remember my mom always spruced up and paid more attention to a young cute man who was an exercise therapist. No kidding; try it.

- My dad loves pretty table settings. He always enjoyed using different dishes and having the table decorated with pretty flowers. Have a surprise "tea party" and sometimes add scotch. It helps.

- If your parents no longer drive, make a weekly outing together to the grocery store. It becomes something they look forward to.

- Get them a pet or even easier, bring your pet for a visit. It's amazing what love a dog brings.

- If you can afford it, it's a wonderful gift to you and your elderly parent to hire a caregiver to help with bathing and bathroom needs. It helps to maintain everyone's dignity.

- Arrange for visitors. Lots of people would love to come for a visit if you make it known that visitors are welcome. Find the best time of your parent's day and schedule guests appropriately.

- If they love baseball, watch baseball. If they love golf, watch golf. If they want to play cards, find the time and make it a "regular" date.

- FaceTime old friends. They all may be housebound, but it's a kick to watch them interact.

- Share news about family members' jobs, relationships, accomplishments. It might just bring back some personal memories for your older parent and spark a conversation from their past.

- It may also be a good idea to withhold some information; in conversation, I was talking to my dad about an employee issue, and he fixated on it for days. I was just "talking"—but he didn't need to know about it. Be selective in your conversations.

- Make your parents a favorites list on their mobile phone to help them easily reach family and friends without needing to search.

- For a special birthday, have all the kids and grandkids write a letter sharing how much Grandma or Grandpa means to them. Place all the letters in a folder or, better yet, a scrapbook with photos so they can read them over and over again.

- Keep an eye on weight and nutrition. When my mom had trouble keeping on weight, I mixed Starbucks Frappuccino with Boost, which added at least five hundred calories any time I could get my mom to drink it.

- An electric recliner is a wonderful thing. Enlarge the size of the TV set without asking. It makes a demonstrable difference. Record a bunch of favorite shows. Don't assume they will tell you the remote is too difficult.

- Be aware of changes in Medicare and help parents navigate coverage when they are being treated for illness or injuries. For example, if staying at a hospital under "observation care" (meaning that patients are not well enough to go home but not sick enough to be admitted), patients will likely have higher out-of-pocket expenses and fewer Medicare benefits.

Most importantly, love them…
just love them.

♥♥♥

CHAPTER 10

Favorite Quotes

I save every GREAT quote I read, whether it's in a book or magazine or on a poster. My list of favorites would fill this book. I've chosen just a few to share—and as I read over them now, I see that they all pertain to the things I hold most dear: family, leadership, friendship, and service to others.

I've attributed as many as I can; but some just seem to be in the air, and I apologize if I've neglected to give credit to any of the sages who first coined them. I thank them for their wisdom.

I've learned that people will forget what you said, people will forget what you did, but people will never forget how you made them feel.

~ Maya Angelou

Anyone who thinks sitting in church can make you a Christian must also think that sitting in a garage can make you a car.

~ Garrison Keillor

The winners in life think constantly in terms of I can, I will, and I am. Losers, on the other hand, concentrate their waking thoughts on what they should have or would have done, or what they can't do.

~ Denis Waitley

Smile through the rain...it's not what life gives you, it's how you handle it.

Try to be a rainbow in someone's cloud.

~ Maya Angelou

Everything that irritates us about others can lead us to an understanding of ourselves.

~ Carl Jung

If you can, help others; if you cannot do that, at least do not harm them.

~ Dalai Lama

Have courage for the great sorrows in life and patience for the small ones; and when you have laboriously accomplished your daily task, go to sleep in peace. God is awake.

~ Victor Hugo

Let your life be your message.

~ Mahatma Gandhi

By the time a woman realizes her mother was right, she has a daughter who thinks she's wrong.

We make a living by what we get, but we make a life by what we give.

~ Winston Churchill

Folks are usually about as happy as they make their minds up to be.

~ Abraham Lincoln

Be silly, be honest, be kind.

Enjoy the little things, for one day you may look back and realize they were the big things.

~ Robert Brault

People react better to feeling the heat than to seeing the light.

We can only be said to be alive in those moments when our hearts are conscious of our treasures.

~ Thornton Wilder

Hire character. Train skill.

~ Peter Schutz

The true test of a man's character is what he does when no one is watching.

~John Wooden

I truly believe that everything that we do and everyone that we meet is put in our path for a purpose. There are no accidents; we're all teachers—if we're willing to pay attention to the lessons we learn, trust our positive instincts and not be afraid to take risks or wait for some miracle to come knocking at our door.

~ Marla Gibbs

Attitude is a little thing that makes a big difference.

~ Winston Churchill

Let us walk in partnership with grace, lighting a path of hope for others.

~ Joanne Smith

Winning means you're willing to go longer, work harder, and give more than anyone else.

~ Vince Lombardi

We must let go of the life we have planned, so as to accept the one that is waiting for us.

~ Joseph Campbell

Ultimately, leadership is not about glorious crowning acts. It's about keeping your team focused on a goal and motivated to do their best to achieve it, especially when the stakes are high and the consequences really matter. It is about laying the groundwork for others' success, and then standing back and letting them shine.

~ Chris Hadfield

Faith is believing in things when common sense tells you not to.

~ George Seaton

A friendship founded on business is better than a business founded on friendship.

~ John D. Rockefeller

Success is a lousy teacher. It seduces smart people into thinking they can't lose.

~ Bill Gates

In any moment of decision, the best thing you can do is the right thing, the next best thing is the wrong thing, and the worst thing you can do is nothing.

~ Theodore Roosevelt

Peace. It does not mean to be in a place where there is no noise, trouble, or hard work. It means to be in the midst of those things and still be calm in your heart.

Watch your thoughts, for they become words;
Watch your words, for they become actions;
Watch your actions, for they become habits;
Watch your habits, for they become character;
Watch your character, for it becomes your destiny.

The best luck of all is the luck you make for yourself.

~ Douglas MacArthur

I know God won't give me anything I can't handle. I just wish he didn't trust me so much.

~ Mother Teresa

I believe that if, at the end of it all, according to our abilities, we have done something to make others a little happier, and something to make ourselves a little happier, that is about the best we can do. To make others less happy is a crime. To make ourselves unhappy is where all crime starts. We must try to contribute joy to the world. That is true no matter what our problems, our health, our circumstances. We must try. I didn't always know this, and am happy I lived long enough to find it out.

~ Roger Ebert

Be a hero minus the dorky cape.

Success is no accident. It is hard work, perseverance, learning, studying, sacrifice, and most of all, love of what you are doing or learning to do.

~ Pelé

The last gift a parent can give a child is to die first so that when our time comes they will be first to greet us.

It is during our darkest moments that we must focus to see the light.

~ Aristotle

Ability may take you to the top, but character keeps you there.

Don't cry because it is over, smile because it happened!

~ Dr. Seuss

Never doubt that a small group of thoughtful, committed citizens can change the world. Indeed, it is the only thing that ever has.

~ Margaret Mead

Live with intention. Walk to the edge. Listen hard. Practice wellness. Play with abandon. Laugh. Choose with no regret. Appreciate your friends. Continue to learn. Do what you love. Live as if this is all there is.

~ Mary Anne Radmacher

When you choose joy, you feel good and when you feel good, you do good and when you do good, it reminds others of what joy feels like and it just might inspire them to do the same.

Be yourself. The most important thing you will ever do is become who you were meant to be.

When we feel love and kindness toward others, it not only makes others feel loved and cared for, but it helps us to develop inner happiness and peace.

~ Dalai Lama

A baby is a small member of the family that makes love stronger, days shorter, nights longer, the home happier, clothes shabbier, the past forgotten, and the future worth living for.

No one can make you feel inferior without your consent.

~ Eleanor Roosevelt

Management is efficiency in climbing the ladder of success; leadership determines whether the ladder is leaning against the right wall.

~ Stephen Covey

Closing Thoughts

A few closing thoughts: This has been an adventure...sometimes fun, sometimes a little hard as I revisited the tough parts of my life. And once I wrote one story, twenty more would pop into my head. I have a list of hundreds of stories that did not make the book, and my family, who have read pieces and parts as I wrote them, keep reminding me of a few more. But the book is already much longer than I ever envisioned, so I elected to not write about a bunch of other important things as each of them would have taken a chapter in itself.

It is impossibly tough to lose a family member to drugs—and the stories are endless—but I am not sure I have all that much "wisdom" to pass along. My divorce came complete with many wisdoms, but my ex-husband and I share three great kids so I chose not to go there. I wish the business chapter had more room as half of the stories I did not write are about business and the boards on which I have had the privilege to serve. Losing a baby at seven-plus months' gestation was impossible (and with my daughter, Liz, the pain returned when one of her pregnancies was terminated after her medical team found "no heartbeat"). I could have told you how NOT to speak with your friends who have lost children—there are not many helpful, positive things you can say about that. Anything you might say hurts, so just stay with hugs. I also did not spend a lot of time on the many lessons I have learned about passing along wealth. My mom had COPD for ten long years, and I could have told you many of the ways I learned to change my life—rather than trying to change hers—as this serious illness progressed and I realized I needed to make accommodations. We could talk about the drunken housekeeper who helped raise me and my siblings—but then again, let's not.

If any of you is the child of the founder or owner of a business and you work in the family company, write me a note. I am happy to share the hundreds of ups and downs and misconceptions. I would say, "Hang in there and prove your worth." That will eventually make the difference in the respect accorded to you. But frankly, the assumptions are not fair, so simply smile and carry on. There were so many new lessons learned on starting up Enchanted Backpack, but the book was almost finished, so those made the "not now" list. I will say it is a hugely rewarding project, and it is fun to see your charitable money touch people directly.

The wonderful part of having a diverse family is the joy and understanding that comes with tolerance of other people's views. My dad was raised Jewish, but his father was not religious at all. My mom was Episcopalian and my first cousins are Catholic. My sister is very spiritual but does not embrace religion. My brother turned to Christianity. I married a man (now my ex) who is Jewish, but we celebrated the joy of all the holidays—including Christmas and Easter. Bobby, the love of my life, was Catholic. My children had bar and bat mitzvahs, but two of my kids married Catholics and one married a Protestant. All my grandchildren have been christened or baptized, but no one is declaring yet how the babies will be raised. The wisdoms are many as they relate to inclusion and prejudice, but this whole topic is for another time. I am most grateful to God for all our many blessings, and we will continue to figure things out.

The funny thing about a book like this is that everyone has important concepts and lessons they can share. So much of life lived—so many good times and times of pain—all come with "wisdoms." Many people have asked me what comes next. Will I do a "Book Two" or will I share more lessons on Facebook? Why don't I create a place where people can share their best lessons? The answer is that I simply don't know. I am not a writer, and writing is not my life. But what has been pretty magical is hearing all the stories from other folks who were exposed to a few of the early stories. So, we have created a simple website (gatherasyougo.com), and I would love to hear from you. Hopefully you have taken something positive from reading *Gather as You Go*. If you care to share some of your best wisdoms, let me know. It might just be fun to share them.

C.L.B.

Acknowledgments

The writing of this book took over the lives of people in my office. I am grateful to my assistant, Kathie Anderson, for always being there and ready at any time to help. My thanks to Christa Bolt and Liz Pietka for their incredible organizational skills, patience, and candor. They kept me on track, pushed back when my words weren't clear, and supported and encouraged me throughout the writing process. The majority of photographs were the work of Glenn Hettinger. And so many of my party themes, gifts, and table designs were executed in partnership with my friend and teammate, Marty Whealy...thank you will never be enough. Amy Stanec and Kirsten Sevig's creativity lends the charm, look, and feel to a very difficult project in which one chapter called for professionalism, another dealt with tragedy, and yet another was lighthearted fun. I thank all these people for their over-the-top efforts to make this process something I could handle and enjoy, while still trying to live my life and run our business.

One person stands out above all others: Dan Stone. Dan has been in my life for many years, initially as vice president of corporate communications at Alberto, where he became my partner in many of Alberto's real challenges. And this last year, he helped me edit this book: he added words when I couldn't come up with the right ones. He calls my writing "Carol speak," and to this day, he is not sure what this book is about or if it should have been written—but that did not stop him from helping me, day or night, no matter what the question or issue. Dan is a wonderful friend to me and to my family. He is the best, and my thanks will never be enough. Thank you, Dan—you mean the world to all of us.

My family is my reason for being, as I am sure you have "gathered": my kids and their wonderful spouses, my grandkids, my sister, my nephew and his partner, Tom, and lessons from my parents all make me who I am. Thank you from the bottom of my heart for all that you are and for all you help me to be.

And to my friends who have supported me through all the ups and downs: words will never capture how important you are to my life and well-being. I hope I have helped you as you have moved along life's path, because you have surely helped me. My heartfelt appreciation to you all.

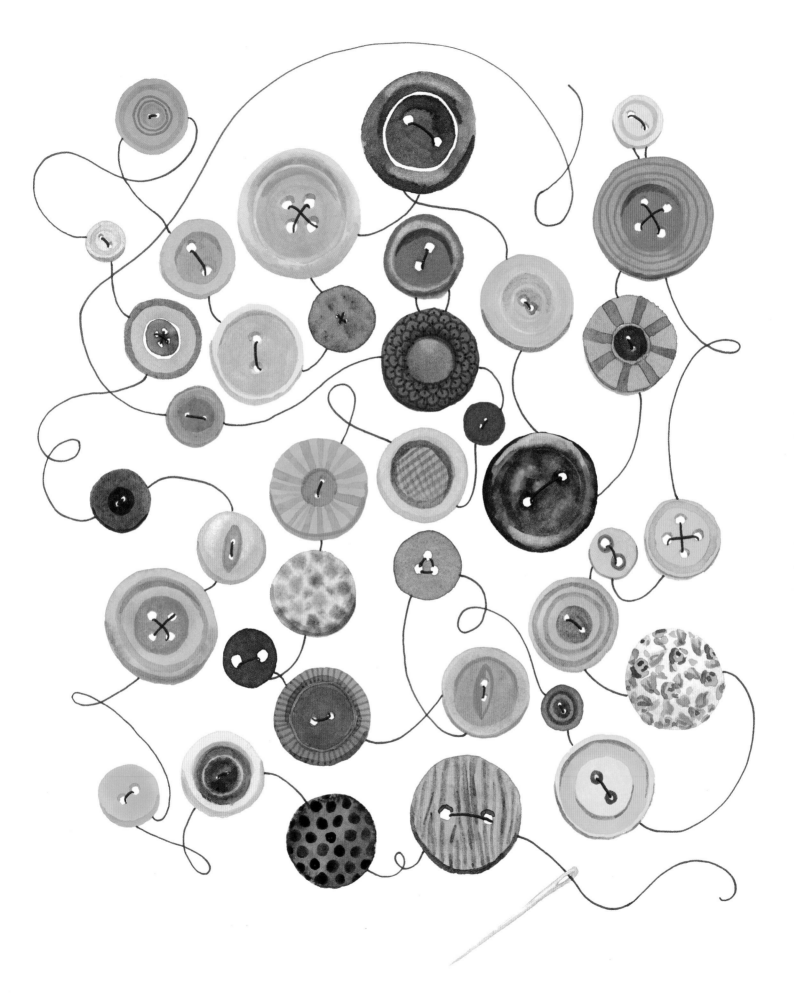

NOTES

FOR A FEW MORE STORIES
AND PHOTOS VISIT:

Gather AS YOU GO.COM

 @gatherasyougo